EROS & EQUUS

EROS & EQUUS

A Passion for the Horse

EDITED BY LAURA CHESTER
PHOTOGRAPHS BY DONNA DEMARI

Willow Creek Press

With special thanks to our editor, Andrea Donner, at Willow Creek Press, who helped see this project through with her good will and creative vision.

Published by Willow Creek Press
P.O. Box 147, Minocqua, Wisconsin 54548

Library of Congress Cataloging-in-Publication Data:

Eros & equus : a passion for the horse / compiled by Laura Chester ; photographs by Donna DeMari.
        p. cm.
   ISBN 1-59543-388-0 (hardcover : alk. paper)
   1. Horses--Literary collections. 2. Human-animal relationships--Literary collections. I. Title: Eros and equus. II. Chester, Laura. III. DeMari, Donna.
   PS509.H67E76 2006
   810.8'036296655--dc22
                                                           2006003991

Printed in Canada

With love to my Dad,
John DeMari, who brought horses into my world

In memory of my father, George Chester,
an incorrigible equestrian

God forbid that I should go to any heaven in which there are no horses.
—R.B. Cuninghame-Graham

CONTENTS

QUIVER
wild joys of Riding

LATHER
Eros & Equus

YONDER
Heartbreak & Haven

INTRODUCTION

As a child, I found the greatest times of togetherness riding alone with my father—off through the open fields of Wisconsin—off into the dairy wind, linked in spirit on horseback. Often we remained quiet, lost in our own calm world that had the dry sweet smell of oats ready for harvest. Pushing through corn stalks on the edge of a field, sneaking through wired-up fences, I became privy to secret trails, certain spots where accidents had happened. It all became a legend in my childish mind, and I was now part of the story, rescued from town and that indoor world of crock-pots and kitchen knives. Out on the trail we were free, part of nature, whisking the heads and rumps of our mounts, so they knew we were not so unlike them.

On occasion, Popi brought a bullwhip along on our rides, wanting some real excitement. He liked to get into the pasture and stir up the herd. This kind of spree made me anxious, yet still I admired my father's bravado—wading across whitewater, sliding down embankments, riding down the middle of railroad tracks.

Popi's barn held a motley crew of llamas, ponies, and Thoroughbreds bought off the track (obviously not winners). People often offered him their rejects and he never looked a gift-horse in the mouth, though he did have one or two favorites, and Merlin was one of them. Once when he wanted to give me a piece of jewelry, he took me into the stall of this dappled Arabian (a horse I considered too small for my Dad), and there around Merlin's neck hung a golden chain necklace for me.

Bunko, an Indian pony, was my first "true love." His white blond mane matched my hair exactly. Later, I fell for a chestnut with a white blaze. "Why this horse," my grandmother asked me. "Because I love him," I said, and my breath made a whiteness. I could hardly believe that my heart had been heard.

Perhaps boys did replace my horse crazy streak for a while, but I didn't appreciate the comment that girls who ride only want sex. Maybe we wanted "a dream smell of stables—the sensation of gripping a mane—the unrestrained feeling of utter freedom when riding out in the morning." On horseback we were fully alive!

In our forties, Donna and I both found our dream horses, Zwen and Nashotah, both of them warmbloods, while my father babied Greystone, his enormous Trakehner, hardly the bomb-proof ride a seventy-five year old gentleman should have been riding with his granddaughters. All Popi could remember was the deafening sound of corn stalks flattening before he fell. The experience earned him an iron arm with seventeen screws but never an iron hand.

Even after recovering from this accident, Popi didn't stay away from his horses. Riding always provided a good opportunity to introduce young, attractive men and women to his sport of choice, for there's nothing like a rendezvous on horseback—an activity which is sensual by nature, alerting the adrenals, exciting the blood. Indeed, Eros & Equus have always been linked in my mind.

The exquisite photographs of Donna DeMari are full of a similar energy and passion. For over two decades, photographer DeMari has been shooting equine images with her special sensitivity, catching the quirky, unexpected detail of mane, muzzle, haunch, and eye, always making it feel immediate, naturally elegant, never posed. Whether it is a rearing stallion or a collected dressage horse, these portraits capture the true artistry of the horse.

The literary material fell naturally into three sections—from the youthful, exuberant wild joys of riding, to more erotic and sensual passages, to the heartbreak and haven of the older years. Whether it's a band of wild girls racing their horses through a river, an old gentleman guiding the proud flesh of his prized stallion home, a naked woman swept up into the saddle of a *bandito*, or a drunken father protecting his daughter's blind horse from the gun, these pieces are as beautiful and moving as the animals they describe.

Lucy Grealy captures the magic of being overcome by the Eros of Equus: "Best of all was when I happened to find him lying down in his stall. Carefully, so as not to spook him, I'd creep in and lie down on top of his giant body, his great animal heat and breath rising up to swallow my own smaller heat and less substantial air." Certainly, it is our pleasure to bring this visual and literary work together here. Hopefully you too will fall under a similar spell.

—Laura Chester

QUIVER

Wild Joys of Riding

O thou, my milk-white pony,
whose coat is as the moonbeams of
this autumn night,
carry me like a bird through the air.

—Murasaki Shikabu

From: NATIONAL VELVET

Enid Bagnold

*V*elvet's dreams were blowing about the bed. They were made of cloud but had the shape of horses. Sometimes she dreamt of bits as women dream of jewelry. Snaffles and straights and pelhams and twisted pelhams were hanging, jointed and still in the shadows of a stable, and above them went up the straight, damp, oiled lines of leathers and cheek straps. The weight of a shining bit and the delicacy of the leather above it was what she adored. Sometimes she walked down an endless cool alley in summer, by the side of the gutter in the old red brick floor. On her left and right were open stalls made of dark wood and the buttocks of the bay horses shone like mahogany all the way down. The horses turned their heads to look at her as she walked. They had black manes hanging like silk as the thick necks turned. These dreams blew and played round her bed in the night and the early hours of the morning.

She got up while the sisters were sleeping and all the room was full of book-muslin and canaries singing. "How can they sleep!" she said wonderingly when she became aware of the canaries singing so madly. All the sisters lay dreaming of horses. The room seemed full of the shapes of horses. There was almost a dream-smell of stables. As she dressed they were stirring, shifting and tossing in white heaps beneath their cotton bedspreads. The canaries screamed in a long yellow scream, and grew madder. Then Velvet left the room and softly shut the door and passed down into the silence of the cupboard-stairway.

THE YOUNG GIRL DREAMS OF ESCAPE

Lyn Lifshin

of a wild mane her
own hair tangles
with, her thighs
opening for the
horse's warmth.
She will elope
when the rest of
the house is sleeping,
carrots and apples
for her love.

From: SWEET WILLIAM

John Hawkes

But who at Millbank do I remember best? My dam, of course, Molly-Long-Legs, or Molly, the tallest and stateliest brood mare ever put to stallion in the covering yard at Millbank. Not for nothing was she named, since never have I seen a horse with legs as long as my dam's, so long in fact that at the withers she stood more than seventeen hands tall, or as tall as a six-foot man. But she was well proportioned, statuesque, no matter that her exceptionally long legs first caught the eye, and she was deep in the chest, broad and sculpted in the hindquarters, with a large head held always high except when she was nuzzling or nudging me or swinging her eyes about to see why I was so inconsiderate at the teat. She was a big bay, a grand bay, the mare most respected by our other mares and the quickest to agitate our stallions. She had been a great runner and had foaled a handsome crowd of winners before me. And no horse had a blacker mane or tail—the tip of hers literally swept the ground—or a coat of a more lustrous brown, so deep and shiny that Jim was forever saying that she looked as good as Viennese chocolate. And this horse, my gorgeous dam, was placid. Placid! For all her virtues, for all her rippling immensity and the spring in her step, still my dam was placid, even when being put to the most impatient of stallions.

* * *

At least for twenty-one days we stayed together, Molly and I, trotted and cantered together in the cool of the early mornings, lived on the best alfalfa and the sweetest grass, despite the dryness of that summer, and drank from the brook and with the other mares and foals sought the shade of the oaks in the afternoons. I knew that I was Molly's progeny, blood of her blood, a long-legged lively replica of my huge and wondrous dam, and no matter how I frolicked with the other foals or allowed myself to be hugged and petted by Millie, who was forever appearing at the edge of this field or that and calling my name,

her sisters not far behind her, still it was to my placid dam that I returned, not only to tug on the teat, and tug I did, but for the smell of her, the size of her, the reassurance I always knew in her presence that she was mine and I hers, as if her thirteen other foals had never existed. More than any other brood mare on the place, Molly swaddled the pains of labor in the glories of her maternal self. This was her character, her personality, to be the embodiment of that concentrated maternity found only in the horse, and during all the hours of those timeless twenty-one days it was from Molly's maternity that I was never far. Further, if I was born to bliss, as I clearly was, my very act of being born, of taking my rightful place at Millbank, brought still greater bliss since from the hour of my birth my presence as the newborn colt, and its significance, affected every horse and human on our sixty acres. The stable girls hummed to themselves, whistled, giggled for no apparent reason, and turned on their portable radios; Bob, the stable manager, spoke to his charges in a more calming voice than ever; the foals leapt about more gaily than they ever had before my arrival, while the mares took still greater pleasure in their young. Our stallions, whom I rarely saw, were in a constant and handsome state of arousal, though at that time there was not a mare in season. And up at the house a similar condition prevailed so that Jim, the stallion among the Gordon mare and fillies, as naturally I sometimes thought of Jim and Jane and their pretty girls, was heavier of flesh, keener of eye, more active yet also more contented than that always pleasant man had been before my hour, while Jane was fuller, more freckled, more flushed in her small face, even happier than usual. As for Nana, Anna, and Millicent, they could not keep away from me, though it was little Millie who loved me most.

The sound of lemon-colored grains of oats in a bucket, the song of the brook, the steady breeze that had blown since I was first able to breathe the air, to drink Molly's milk, to run, to try my voice, all the sights and signs of well-being that spread from Molly and me to our world at large, and above all my dam herself, placid handsome creature emblematic of everlasting equine life—it was time out of time, pastoral time as Jim drove the orange tractor in the distance and the ping of a horse's shoe on rock rang ever after, never fading in the warm light of day or darkening night.

From: THE GYPSIES

Yan Yoors

*Th*e day of the horse fair we young ones got up before dawn. We braided the horses' shiny manes and tails, tied them with flame-red ribbons and set out before breakfast to take the herd to town. I went with Kore and Nanosh and Zurka, the son of Tshukurka, and Yayal, and several other boys, riding bareback, surrounded by fast-trotting, nervous, rearing, kicking horses, enveloped by a cloud of dust. For hours while the sun was climbing the skies we rode like this toward the city, drowned in the sounds of the pounding of hoofs and the quick short crack of whips, the whinnying of the horses and the high-pitched yells of the boys urging them on. The sweat of the horses smelled strong and the sun grew hot. The wild ride and the continuous noise and the feel of the broad muscular flanks yielding to the nervous pressure of my knees and heels gave me an intoxicating feeling of power.

PORTRAIT OF A GIRL AND HER HORSE

Jana Harris

I think of you often,
my sorrel Goldico horse.
You, who were the red
of the ribbed evening sky.
Hot summer days
belly-heavy in foal
we rode past the men
at the rock quarry
unafraid
rode through the aphrodisiac fields
of new mown hay
watching the flight of eagles
tormented by crows.
Behind the arch of your neck
I rode
to the rocks of the Clackamas River
worshiping
the bronzed power of your thighs.
Chariot horse
you swam the white water,
carried me sand-bar to sand-bar
til we were numb.
And those currents that drove us
across the mossed-granite rocks,
though they were silent
you knew them like eels
knew them
like you knew the paths of the sun.
Goldico
those were summers with nights
too thick for sleeping,
nights where I drowned
the dark spots of my soul
in that river
drifting downstream.

From: MEMOIRS OF A FOX-HUNTING MAN

Siegfried Sassoon

I noticed for the first time another boy of about my own age. Dixon was watching him approvingly. Evidently this was a boy to be imitated, and my own unsophisticated eyes already told me that. He was near enough to us for me to be able to observe him minutely. A little aloof from the large riders round him, he sat easily, but very upright, on a corky chestnut pony with a trimmed stump of a tail and a neatly 'hogged' neck.

Reconstructing that far-off moment, my memory fixes him in a characteristic attitude. Leaning slightly forward from the waist, he straightens his left leg and scrutinizes it with an air of critical abstraction. He seems to be satisfied with his smart buff breeches and natty brown gaiters. Everything he has on is neat and compact. He carries a small crop with a dark leather thong, which he flicks at a tuft of dead grass in a masterly manner. An air of self-possessed efficiency begins with his black bowler hat, continues in his neatly tied white stock, and gets its finishing touch in the short, blunt, shining spurs on his black walking boots. (I was greatly impressed by the fact that he wore spurs.) All his movements were controlled and modest, but there was a suggestion of arrogance in the steady, unrecognizing stare which he gave me when he became conscious that I was looking at him so intently. Our eyes met, and his calm scrutiny reminded me of my own deficiencies in dress. I shifted uneasily in my saddle, and the clumsy unpresentable old hunting-crop fell out of my hand. Dismounting awkwardly to pick it up, I wished that it, also, had a thong (though this would make the double reins more difficult to manage), and I hated my silly jockey-cap and the badly fitting gaiters which pinched my legs and always refused to remain in the correct position (indicated by Dixon). When I had scrambled up on to Sheila again—a feat which I could only just accomplish without assistance—I felt what a poor figure I must be cutting in Dixon's eyes while he compared me with that other boy, who had himself turned away with a slight smile and was now soberly following the dappled clustering pack and its attendant red-coats as they disappeared over the green rising ground on their way to Hoath Wood.

From: RIDING IN THE RESERVE

Isak Dinesen

I rode into the Masai Reserve. I had to cross the river to get there; riding on, I got into the Game Reserve in a quarter of an hour. It had taken me some time, while I had lived on the farm, to find a place where I could get over the river on horseback: the descent was stony, and the slope up the other side very steep, but "once in,—how the delighted spirit pants for joy."

Here lay before you a hundred miles' gallop over grass and open undulating land; there was not a fence nor a ditch, and no road. There was no human habitation except the Masai villages, and those were deserted half the year, when the great wanderers took themselves and their herds off to other pastures. There were low thorn trees regularly spread over the plain, and long deep valleys with dry riverbeds of big flat stones, where you had to find a deer-path here and there to take you across. After a little while you became aware of how still it was out here. Now, looking back on my life in Africa, I feel that it might altogether be described as the existence of a person who had come from a rushed and noisy world, into a still country.

A little before the rains, the Masai burn off the old dry grass, and while the plains are thus lying black and waste they are unpleasant to travel on: you will get the black charred dust, which the hoofs of your horse raise, all over you and into your eyes, and the burnt grass-stalks are sharp as glass; your dogs get their feet cut on them. But when the rains come, and the young green grass is fresh on the plains, you feel as if riding upon springs, and the horse gets a little mad with the pleasantness. The various kinds of gazelles come to the green places to graze, and there look like toy animals stood upon a billiard table. You may ride into a herd of Eland; the mighty peaceful beasts will let you get close to them before they start trotting off, their long horns streaming backwards over their raised necks, the large loose flaps of breastskin, that make them look square, swaying as they jog. They seem to have come out of an old Egyptian epitaph, but there they have been ploughing the fields, which gives them a familiar and domesticated air. The Giraffe keep farther away in the Reserve.

At times, in the first month of the rains, a sort of wild white fragrant Pink flowers so richly all over the Reserve that at a distance the plains look patched with snow.

From: SPARKS

Laura Chester

Up the dirt hill we become horses—all girls
crazed creatures. Riding along then—wildly racing
up the dirt mound—King of the Hill, not queen we go—
down *Down* the slope of the hard-pack, throwing manes
and kicking out. Horse legs bracing. "Too bad you didn't
inherit your mother's." *Uh*-oh. I stormed the hill and
Reigned Supreme. Stomped my loafer hoof (and *screamed!*

THE SUMMER OF THE BEAUTIFUL WHITE HORSE

William Saroyan

One day back there in the good old days when I was nine and the world was full of every imaginable kind of magnificence, and life was still a delightful and mysterious dream, my cousin Mourad, who was considered crazy by everybody who knew him except me, came to my house at four in the morning and woke me up by tapping on the window of my room.

Aram, he said.

I jumped out of bed and looked out the window.

I couldn't believe what I saw.

It wasn't morning yet, but it was summer and with daybreak not many minutes around the corner of the world it was light enough for me to know I wasn't dreaming.

My cousin Mourad was sitting on a beautiful white horse.

I stuck my head out of the window and rubbed my eyes.

Yes, he said in Armenian. It's a horse. You're not dreaming. Make it quick if you want a ride.

I knew my cousin Mourad enjoyed being alive more than anybody else who had ever fallen into the world by mistake, but this was more than even I could believe.

In the first place, my earliest memories had been memories of horses and my first longings had been longings to ride.

This was the wonderful part.

In the second place, we were poor.

This was the part that wouldn't permit me to believe what I saw.

We were poor. We had no money. Our whole tribe was poverty-stricken. Every branch of the Garoghlanian family was living in the most amazing and comical poverty in the world. Nobody could understand where we ever got money enough to keep us with food in our bellies, not even the old men of the family. Most important of all, though, we were famous for our honesty. We had been famous for our honesty for something like eleven centuries, even when we had been the wealth-

iest family in what we liked to think was the world. We were proud first, honest next, and after that we believed in right and wrong. None of us would take advantage of anybody in the world, let alone steal.

Consequently, even though I could see the horse, so magnificent; even though I could *smell* it, so lovely; even though I could *hear* it breathing, so exciting; I couldn't *believe* the horse had anything to do with my cousin Mourad or with me or with any of the other members of our family, asleep or awake, because I *knew* my cousin Mourad couldn't have bought the horse, and if he couldn't have *bought* it he must have *stolen* it, and I refused to believe he had stolen it.

No member of the Garoghlanian family could be a thief.

I stared first at my cousin and then at the horse. There was a pious stillness and humor in each of them which on the one hand delighted me and on the other frightened me.

Mourad, I said, where did you steal this horse?

Leap out of the window, he said, if you want a ride.

It was true, then. He *had* stolen the horse. There was no question about it. He had come to invite me to ride or not, as I chose.

Well, it seemed to me stealing a horse for a ride was not the same thing as stealing something else, such as money. For all I knew, maybe it wasn't stealing at all. If you were crazy about horses the way my cousin Mourad and I were, it wasn't stealing. It wouldn't become stealing until we offered to sell the horse, which of course I knew we would never do.

Let me put on some clothes, I said.

All right, he said, but hurry.

I leaped into my clothes.

I jumped down to the yard from the window and leaped up onto the horse behind my cousin Mourad.

That year we lived at the edge of town, on Walnut Avenue. Behind our house was the country: vineyards, orchards, irrigation ditches, and country roads. In less than three minutes we were on Olive Avenue, and then the horse began to trot. The air was new and lovely to breathe. The feel of the horse running was wonderful. My cousin Mourad who was considered one of the craziest members of our family began to sing. I mean, he began to roar.

Every family has a crazy streak in it somewhere, and my cousin Mourad was considered the natural descendant of the crazy streak in our tribe. Before him was our uncle Khosrove, an enormous man with a powerful head of black hair and the largest mustache in the San Joaquin Valley, a man so furious in temper, so irritable, so impatient that he stopped anyone from talking by roaring, *It is no harm; pay no attention to it.*

That was all, no matter what anybody happened to be talking about. Once it was his own son Arak running eight blocks to the barber shop where his father was having his mustache trimmed to tell him their house was on fire. The man Khosrove sat up in the chair and roared, It is no harm; pay no attention to it. The barber said, But the boy says your house is on fire. So Khosrove roared, Enough, it is no harm, I say.

My cousin Mourad was considered the natural descendant of this man, although Mourad's father was Zorab, who was practical and nothing else. That's how it was in our tribe. A man could be the father of his son's flesh, but that did not mean that he was also the father of his spirit. The distribution of the various kinds of spirit of our tribe had been from the beginning capricious and vagrant.

We rode and my cousin Mourad sang. For all anybody knew we were still in the old country where, at least according to our neighbors, we belonged. We let the horse run as long as it felt like running.

At last my cousin Mourad said, Get down. I want to ride alone.

Will you let me ride alone? I said.

That is up to the horse, my cousin said. Get down.

The *horse* will let me ride, I said.

We shall see, he said. Don't forget that I have a way with a horse.

Well, I said, any way you have with a horse, I have also.

For the sake of your safety, he said, let us hope so. Get down.

All right, I said, but remember you've got to let me try to ride alone.

I got down and my cousin Mourad kicked his heels into the horse and shouted, *Vazire*, run. The horse stood on its hind legs, snorted, and burst into a fury of speed that was the loveliest thing I had ever seen. My cousin Mourad raced the horse across a field of dry grass to an irrigation ditch, crossed the ditch on the horse, and five minutes later returned, dripping wet.

The sun was coming up.

Now it's my turn to ride, I said.

My cousin Mourad got off the horse.

Ride, he said.

I leaped to the back of the horse and for a moment knew the awfulest fear imaginable. The horse did not move.

Kick into his muscles, my cousin Mourad said. What are you waiting for? We've got to take him back before everybody in the world is up and about.

I kicked into the muscles of the horse. Once again it reared and snorted. Then it began to run. I didn't know what to do. Instead of running across the field to the irrigation ditch the horse ran down the road to the vineyard of Dikran Halabian where it began to leap over vines. The horse leaped over seven vines before I fell. Then it continued running.

My cousin Mourad came running down the road.

I'm not worried about you, he shouted. We've got to get that horse. You go this way and I'll go this way. If you come upon him, be kindly. I'll be near.

I continued down the road and my cousin Mourad went across the field toward the irrigation ditch.

It took him half an hour to find the horse and bring him back.

All right, he said, jump on. The whole world is awake now.

What will we do? I said.

Well, he said, we'll either take him back or hide him until tomorrow morning.

He didn't sound worried and I knew he'd hide him and not take him back. Not for a while, at any rate.

Where will you hide him? I said.

I know a place, he said.

How long ago did you steal this horse? I said.

It suddenly dawned on me that he had been taking these early morning rides for some time and had come for me this morning only because he knew how much I longed to ride.

Who said anything about stealing a horse? he said.

Anyhow, I said, how long ago did you begin riding every morning?

EROS & EQUUS 33

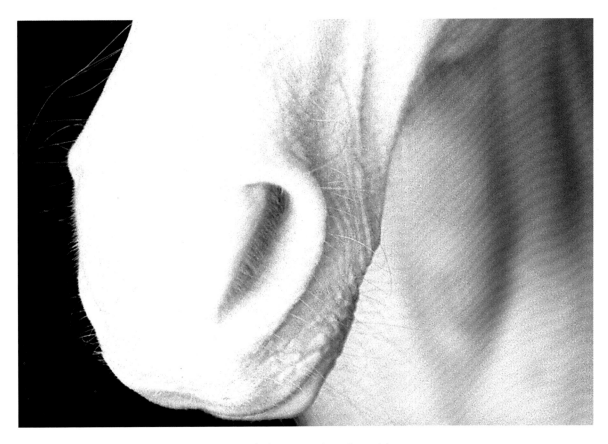

Not until this morning, he said.

Are you telling the truth? I said.

Of course not, he said, but if we are found out, that's what you're to say. I don't want both of us to be liars. All you know is that we started riding this morning.

All right, I said.

He walked the horse quietly to the barn of a deserted vineyard which at one time had been the pride of a farmer named Fetvajian. There were some oats and dry alfalfa in the barn.

We began walking home.

It wasn't easy, he said, to get the horse to behave so nicely. At first it wanted to run wild, but as I've told you, I have a way with a horse. I can get it to want to do anything I want it to do. Horses understand me.

How do you do it? I said.

I have an understanding with a horse, he said.

Yes, but what sort of an understanding? I said.

A simple and honest one, he said.

Well, I said, I wish I knew how to reach an understanding like that with a horse.

You're still a small boy, he said. When you get to be thirteen you'll know how to do it.

I went home and ate a hearty breakfast.

That afternoon my uncle Khosrove came to our house for coffee and cigarettes. He sat in the parlor, sipping and smoking and remembering the old country. Then another visitor arrived, a farmer named John Byro, an Assyrian who, out of loneliness, had learned to speak Armenian. My mother brought the lonely visitor coffee and tobacco and he rolled a cigarette and sipped and smoked, and then at last, sighing sadly, he said, My white horse which was stolen last month is still gone. I cannot understand it.

My uncle Khosrove became very irritated and shouted, It's no harm. What is the loss of a horse? Haven't we all lost the homeland? What is this crying over a horse?

That may be all right for you, a city dweller, to say, John Byro said, but what of my surrey? What good is a surrey without a horse?

Pay no attention to it, my uncle Khosrove roared.

I walked ten miles to get here, John Byro said.

You have legs, my uncle Khosrove shouted.

My left leg pains me, the farmer said.

Pay no attention to it, my uncle Khosrove roared.

That horse cost me sixty dollars, the farmer said.

I spit on money, my uncle Khosrove said.

He got up and stalked out of the house, slamming the screen door.

My mother explained.

He has a gentle heart, she said. It is simply that he is homesick and such a large man.

The farmer went away and I ran over to my cousin Mourad's house.

He was sitting under a peach tree, trying to repair the hurt wing of a young robin which could not fly. He was talking to the bird.

What is it? he said.

The farmer, John Byro, I said. He visited our house. He wants his horse. You've had it a month. I want you to promise not to take it back until I learn to ride.

It will take you a year to learn to ride, my cousin Mourad said.

We could keep the horse a year, I said.

My cousin Mourad leaped to his feet.

What? he roared. Are you inviting a member of the Garoghlanian family to steal? The horse must go back to its true owner.

When? I said.

In six months at the latest, he said.

He threw the bird into the air. The bird tried hard, almost fell twice, but at last flew away, high and straight.

Early every morning for two weeks my cousin Mourad and I took the horse out of the barn of the deserted vineyard where we were hiding it and rode it, and every morning the horse, when it was my turn to ride alone, leaped over grapevines and small trees and threw me and ran away. Nevertheless, I hoped in time to learn to ride the way my cousin Mourad rode.

One morning on the way to Fetvajian's deserted vineyard we ran into the farmer John Byro who was on his way to town.

Let me do the talking, my cousin Mourad said. I have a way with farmers.

Good morning, John Byro, my cousin Mourad said to the farmer.

The farmer studied the horse eagerly.

Good morning, sons of my friends, he said. What is the name of your horse?

My Heart, my cousin Mourad said in Armenian.

A lovely name, John Byro said, for a lovely horse. I could swear it is the horse that was stolen from me many weeks ago. May I look into its mouth?

Of course, Mourad said.

The farmer looked into the mouth of the horse.

Tooth for tooth, he said. I would swear it is my horse if I didn't know your parents. The fame of your family for honesty is well known to me. Yet the horse is the twin of my horse. A suspicious man would believe his eyes instead of his heart. Good day, my young friends.

Good day, John Byro, my cousin Mourad said.

Early the following morning we took the horse to John Byro's vine-yard and put it in the barn. The dogs followed us around without mak-ing a sound.

The dogs, I whispered to my cousin Mourad. I thought they would bark.

They would at somebody else, he said. I have a way with dogs.

My cousin Mourad put his arms around the horse, pressed his nose into the horse's nose, patted it, and then we went away.

That afternoon John Byro came to our house in his surrey and showed my mother the horse that had been stolen and returned.

I do not know what to think, he said. The horse is stronger than ever. Better-tempered, too. I thank God.

My uncle Khosrove, who was in the parlor, became irritated and shouted, Quiet, man, quiet. Your horse has been returned. Pay no attention to it.

HORSES AND GIRLS

Amy Gerstler

In the pasture at dusk
when the day's last light strikes
him just right, the dun pony
turns burnished gold for a moment,
standing alone by the fence,
nibbling timothy.

A pony's quick nip is better than any kiss.
Some ponies are ticklish. Being touched
too lightly upsets them, makes their skin shiver.
Others are shy about revealing their teeth.
We braid their tails, oil their hooves,
brush them till their coats glow.
Our first taste of flight comes astride them,
enveloped in their smell. *Erotic*
is a drowsy, inadequate word. The *t* is dangerous,
a spindle on which a princess pricks
her finger. Then she dies. Printed
in fancy script on engraved invitations,
erotic's six letters cannot do justice
to horses' shoulders and swiftness,
to the sensation of gripping a mane.
Fred Astaire never danced like this.
No man ever won a steeplechase
after swimming ashore from a shipwreck.
But my brave stallion did.

My horse is the color of volcanic glass. His breath
is a meadow, mown to stubble and pitched into a furnace.
There's nothing thrilling or fiery about our first names: *Cindy,*
Becky, Nina, Louise, prized for pinkness and giggling.

We demand to be rechristened,
as *Burt's Inferno, Tempest-Tossed,*
Raging Fever, or *Dancethruthenight*.

A horse is a galloping god and a handsome
    dappled villain.
Clomping up your front porch steps, whistling,
    he brings welcome news of the end of a long war.
He's electricity crackling through the veins of autumn leaves.
All wrongs are washed away riding him
    into the rush of a baptismal wind.
He's a Druid priest with a long face, a love of bitter herbs
    and a jagged white star on his forehead.
He's a limping hero of old we hardly recognize
    these late, jaded days:
Odysseus returning to Ithaca disguised as a beggar,
    burrs stuck to his hide and worms furled in his gut.
He's a prince whispering to each princess in turn:

    We shall exhaust ourselves together.
    We shall be married on horseback.
    A bridle path is just what you always insisted it was,
    a road you take to marry your horse.
    When we are wed I will give you free reign.
    I will snort and nuzzle your neck,
    but retain my ability to speak to you,
    for only you understand me, my truest love.
    Only you will I allow to cinch up my saddle,
    and place the sacred, clinking bit
    between my teeth.

From: HORSE PEOPLE

Michael Korda

*Th*en, all of a sudden, during a pause between events, a boy of about twelve rode out into the ring on a nice-looking palomino pony. There was nothing special about him—he wore jeans, a Stetson, and a checked western shirt, and his face was set in a serious expression. First he walked around the ring, while the noise and the hubbub went on and hardly anybody paid him any notice; then he picked up a trot, and I started to look at him more closely. His back was straight, his legs motionless, the seat of his jeans appeared to be glued to his saddle, and his horse was perfectly "collected," neck high, head tucked in, mouthing the bit nicely, his legs well under him. He was "in the frame," as dressage teachers describe it, and James Fillis, had he been alive and present in Archer City, would have been, I thought, mighty pleased. Here was "complete equilibrium," just as he had defined it, the "energetic, harmonious and light whole" he had sought for all his life, not to speak of fingers holding the reins as dexterous as those of the finest concert pianist.

The boy kept trotting around the ring, so perfectly seated on his horse that he might have passed for an adolescent centaur, while gradually, but very noticeably, the noise level among the spectators decreased, then fell away to silence as the boy picked up a canter. The canter was slow, collected, perfect, as good as anything you might see in the Spanish Riding School in Vienna, and by now the spectators were completely absorbed. Then a largish man rode out into the arena on a dapple-gray quarter horse—the spitting image of Missouri, it occurred to me—and joined the boy, riding stirrup to stirrup with him. It was obvious without being told that he was the boy's father— their features were identical, and he rode with the same easy perfection, making it look completely effortless.

By now you could have heard a pin drop—there wasn't a sound except for the thud of the horse's hooves and their steady breathing. Neither father nor son *did* anything fancy or unusual, a couple of figure eights with a perfectly timed change of lead, but they didn't *need* to do anything fancy; they were simply demonstrating perfection. This was an audience that still had, for the most part, ranching roots. The men might be working in the oil industry now, or driving a semi, or a bulldozer, or keeping a store; most of them probably hadn't been on a horse in years, perhaps not since they were kids themselves, but they were close enough to the past to recognize and respect great horsemanship when they saw it, and to appreciate it the way you might appreciate any other skill displayed perfectly. Many of them probably had fathers, or grandfathers, or uncles, maybe some still living, who had spent their working lives with horses, and for whom a man's seat in the saddle mattered almost more than anything else in defining his place in society, much as it had when Cervantes lived in Spain.

They watched, smoking, or chewing tobacco or gum, transfixed, as if the spectacle before them was somehow ennobling, giving them, in their turn, merely by looking at it and recognizing it for what it was, more dignity than they would ever get on the seat of a bulldozer. Something was happening out there in the ring that was no longer part of their lives and never would be, but which had been, until recently, part of everyone's life around here, and under the bright, buzzing lights, hissing and popping as insects brushed against them and burst into flame, one brief and unmistakable moment was almost religious, a feeling like that of the crowds solemnly watching a procession of *penitentes* in New Mexico, not so far from here, when they carried their huge crucifixes and relics of saints up the steep hills toward Taos. These people, here in Archer City, would not necessarily be impressed by the Spanish Riding School, with its crystal chandeliers and nineteenth-century Hapsburg uniforms, still less by the National Horse Show in Madison Square Garden, with most of the audience in dinner jackets or evening gowns and the riders in their red coats and black velvet hats, but unlike most of the audiences at both these events, they knew the real thing when they saw it, and by their silence they paid homage to it.

TALK

Mary Koncel

You can tell the horse anything. You can tell him about the weather, fancy lace underpants, bored neighbors with fat tender stares. The horse will listen. He'll ease himself into the corner of the stall, flick back an ear, scratch a leg, or toss through his hay. In the pasture, summer wafts between the fence posts, and clover is blooming again. But the horse will stay. You can tell him about your head, how it aches when you see bare trees and remember a red-haired child, pale and breathless in her shadow. The horse'll nod. He will listen as you untangle his forelock, rub his belly, feed him a handful of sugar cubes and maybe a pear. You can tell him that nothing matters to you, nothing. Oh horse, you'll whisper, because you are so happy, because the day is long and the horse is snorting.

From: AUTOBIOGRAPHY OF A FACE

Lucy Grealy

I knew his whole being. There was not one part of his body I could not touch, not one part of his personality I did not know at least as well as my own. When we went on long rides through the woods, I would tell him everything I knew and then explain why I loved him so much, why he was special, different from other horses, how I would take care of him for the rest of my life, never leave him or let anyone harm him. After the ride I would take him to graze in an empty field. I would lie down on his broad bare back and think I was the luckiest girl alive, his weight shifting beneath me as he moved toward the next bite of grass. Sometimes I took him to the stream and laughed as he pawed at the water, screaming in delight when he tried to lie down in it. Best of all was when I happened to find him lying down in his stall. Carefully, so as not to spook him, I'd creep in and lie down on top of his giant body, his great animal heat and breath rising up to swallow my own smaller heat and less substantial air.

A BLESSING

James Wright

Just off the highway to Rochester, Minnesota,
Twilight bounds softly forth on the grass.
And the eyes of those two Indian ponies
Darken with kindness.
They have come gladly out of the willows
To welcome my friend and me.
We step over the barbed wire into the pasture
Where they had been grazing all day, alone.
They ripple tensely, they can hardly contain their happiness
That we have come.
They bow shyly as wet swans. They love each other.
There is no loneliness like theirs.
At home once more,
They begin munching the young tufts of spring in
the darkness.
I would like to hold the slenderer one in my arms,
For she has walked over to me
And nuzzled my left hand.
She is black and white,
Her mane falls wild on her forehead,
And the light breeze moves me to caress her long ear
That is delicate as the skin over a girl's wrist.
Suddenly I realize
That if I stepped out of my body I would break
Into blossom.

From: INNOCENCE IN EXTREMIS

John Hawkes

*Th*en the Old Gentleman gave a flourish with his right hand, curving the open and graceful old hand as might an impresario summoning an actor from his place of concealment in the wings. And in response to his flourish there came a tiny, sprightly clattering of hooves and through the gateway rode a young girl on a small and shapely dappled gray horse. Here was a sight to win them all and audibly they sighed and visibly they leaned forward. The girl, who was the youngest child of the Old Gentleman's eighth son, was the same age as Granny—fourteen—and though she had been shyly present in the chateau since this Deauville family reunion had commenced, she had from time to time caught Uncle Jake's attention when he had seen her firm young face in the candlelight, like a pale petal on a white china dish, or had spied her slipping carefully into seclusion behind a mass of garrulous adults, still he had not been prepared for the vision she now presented to her already grateful audience. She looked like neither boy nor girl or like the best of both. She wore a trim black riding coat, a white stock, black boots and a black skirt that reached to her ankles. Best of all she wore a black silk hat which, befittingly small to suit her little head, nonetheless called to mind the larger and bolder silk hats generally worn by aristocratic men. Her dark brown hair was drawn tightly to her head and arranged in a short plait that barely touched the velvet collar of her coat. Around her silk hat, which was tilted becomingly forward, was tied a white silk ribbon that fluttered down the back of her neck and provided exactly the right touch of freedom and formlessness against the plait of hair. She was wearing gray gloves and riding side-saddle.

As for her horse, its size could not have been more appropriate to the size of its rider or its color and markings more complementary to her costume. The distance between the top of the girl's silk hat and the saddle, which was hidden beneath the skirts of the riding coat, was the same as from the saddle to the brightly varnished black hooves that

were the size of teacups; when the breeze tossed up the gray silken tail in the filmy plume of abandon, the spread tail was a perfect counterpart to the horse's head and neck and rose to the height of the little creature's comely head. The gray mane was so long that it echoed the tail; the black colorations of the horse's legs were like tight stockings that mirrored the prim costume of the rider. The small gray horse looked like a hobbyhorse, its rider like a little man. Yet the horse was filled with the supplest life and no young girl could have sat upon its back more decorously than did the daughter of the Old Gentleman's eighth son. Together they were toy-like and so pretty that even the Old Gentleman in that moment watched his granddaughter with admiration and not the slightest sign of desire.

But the Old Gentleman had orchestrated the young girl's exhibition, for so it was to be, in such a way as to bring to absolute fruition the beauty of the young girl and her steed. He had gone so far as to choose the hour so that when the young girl stopped her horse in the center of the courtyard, as now she did, the sun was at such a distance above the westerly wall as to make fall across the cobblestones the largest and longest possible shadow of horse and rider. He had had the rows of chairs arranged at the eastern end of the courtyard so that his audience faced not only the girl and horse but, more important, the shadow that made them one and the same. He had even instructed his equestrienne to keep the head of her mount facing to the north throughout the performance so that she presented to her audience only her right side and never the left, and by so doing—since both her legs were positioned on the left side of the horse—created for her audience the illusion of a legless rider seated in perfect balance upon her horse. The fact that she appeared to have no legs was to the entire ensemble as was the white ribbon affixed to her hat: the incongruity without which the congruous whole could not have achieved such perfection.

There sat Uncle Jake leaning forward in the front row with his hands on his knees and his mouth open; there before him were the performers, quite motionless but for the fluttering ribbon and the mane and tail stirring in the breeze. With shame he thought of himself and his shaggy and dumpy pony back at Deauville Farms; with helpless

ardor he beheld in the girl and her gray horse a vision of poise such as he thought would never again be his to savor.

The exhibition began: The miniature portrait came to life. The young girl did not move so much as a finger, as far as Uncle Jake could see, but her steed responded to her invisible command: it cocked its right front leg and then the left. And again. The reins were gently curving from the young girl's lowered hands to the silver bit; she was applying no tension to the reins. Now the horse moved sideways three paces, no more and no less, in Uncle Jake's direction, and then returned to its starting place and stopped. Then it took three paces forward and returned. And then the small full-bodied animal began to dance, as did the elongated shadow, and drummed with all four of its pretty hooves on the cobblestones in a medley of pure obedience to the girl it bore. It danced, it drummed, it turned, but never so far as to destroy the illusion of its impossibly legless rider, and all the while the girl disguised as a little man did not vary in any way her pretty posture as the horse continued to captivate hosts and visitors alike in its dance.

Nearly everyone in that audience rode horseback. Most of them were fox hunters. Their lives depended on horses, whether or not they hallooed while hurtling over high fences, and whether or not they loved their massive mounts as much as they did their own children. Some of them secretly feared past injuries and those to come; a few had little aptitude for riding. Yet for all of them their mares and geldings and fillies and stallions were a matter of course like stones in a brook or birds in the boughs. Most of the horses they bred and rode were large, rugged, unruly, brutish beasts of great stamina. The horses raced and hunted, pulled their carriages, carried them ambling through sylvan woods and took them cantering great distances. But little more. So here in the Old Gentleman's courtyard the spectacle of the young equestrienne and her gray horse schooled only in dressage appealed directly to what they knew and to their own relationships to horse and stable yet gave them all a taste of equestrian refinement that stirred them to surprise and pleasure. They had never thought of horsemanship as an art, but here indeed in the dancing horse they could see full well the refinement of an artist's mind.

As they waited, hoping the finals would never come, the Irish matriarch, who for days had regretted that her past refusal to ride with her husband now prevented her from joining the Old Gentleman in the hunting field and consigned her instead to the two-wheeled carriage driven by her mother-in-law and from which she could see little of the old and brave patrician, suddenly found herself constrained to whisper behind her hand to Uncle Jake.

"Jake," she whispered, "mark my words, dear boy. That child is dangerous."

He was stunned. He envied the girl, he likened her to their youngest maid, he loved her, he wanted to become her and take her splendid place on the gray horse, even though he had no use for horses. Surely the girl who might have been his sister could not in any way be sinister, as his mother had said. He was confident that there was nothing sinister about her.

But the Irish matriarch, who was proud of her self-control, did not know why she had been so suddenly stung to spite by a young horsewoman as clearly innocent as her own second son. So quickly she added in a gentler voice: "But she is a beautiful little rider, Jake. You might try to ride as well as she does. It would please your father."

In his relief he smiled, leaned briefly toward the once more reassuring bulk of his mother, and returned to concentrating on the girl and the bobbing and swaying horse.

Then came the finale.

All at once and above the dainty clatter of the hooves, they heard the loud and charming tinkling of a music box. Heads turned, a new and livelier surprise possessed the audience, the fact that they could not discover the source of the music, which was the essence of artificiality, added greatly to the effect. Thanks to its quick and pretty strains that were suggestive of the tips of quills picking silver strings as fine as hair, the horse's dance attained its childlike crescendo while the rider allowed herself the faintest smile. The tempo of the music began to slow, with no distortion of its tinkling notes, and with it slowed the dance of the gray horse. The slower the music, the slower the dance; and just as the even longer spaces between the notes caused each note to stand increasingly alone as if it were to be the only one struck on the scale of poignancy, so the modulation of the horse toward motionlessness brought to a head the lovely aching quality of its movements. Then the music ceased, leaving behind its song in the silence, and the horse and rider grew so still that they might have been waxen figures in an equestrian museum. And then, with a slowness that brought everyone to the edge of his seat, the gray horse bowed. Out went its front legs, down came the head and neck and chest, lower and lower in the greatest possible contrast to the vertical line of the young girl, until the audience could no longer bear the nearly human tribute paid to it by the little horse and broke out in sustained and mellifluous applause. At once the animal returned to its proper stance, the girl laughed, and horse and rider backed out of the courtyard and disappeared through the gate.

NOW THE PASTURES ARE EMPTY

Lyn Lifshin

the mares stand alone in their stalls.
Those who've lost their foals
for the first time, paw the hay,
sniff for something familiar.
Moments before, the barn full of
shrieks and neighing, a dark
truck back firing. Ruffian dug her
tiny feet into the hay, tried to
nuzzle her mare, her long legs black
as the bones of cherry branches.
She was born as the petals opened,
stood close to her mother in the
shade, is gone before light
comes

RIVER GIRLS

Jeanne Dixon

They were late this spring because of the cold. But every year when school lets out and the weather warms up, those pale young girls with stringy brown hair or blond, freckles maybe, their cotton-blend dresses hanging straight to the knee, those country girls with lunch box and thermos—Donna, Ardella, Delphina, and Joyce, and Tootie (if she's not too grown-up), dark-eyed Debbie, tall, shy Johanna with her braces and glasses—all those see-through girls the boys never notice, shed school clothes like snakeskins and take to the rivers on horseback.

Donna rides a pinto, a stocky black and white. Ardella has a common bay, Delphina a blaze-faced sorrel. Tootie's horse is part Belgian, black as soot at midnight. He pulled a loaded stone boat to victory in a pulling match at the Hamilton Creamery Picnic one year, "broke his wind" doing so, and was sold to a canner for dog food. Tootie's dad bought him back. "A darn good kid's horse," her dad said. "Slow and steady. Can't get him out of a trot." The man could not have guessed what wild currents the old horse would swim, what heights he would scramble to, how he'd pace like a hound to the hunt through the quivering light of the river lands.

Appaloosa, buckskin, mouse gray—they gather speed at the first scent of river water. And all the dogs for a mile around hear the clatter of hooves on the graveled lanes and bark to get out and go with them—fat black Labs that slept through the winter by the heater stove, water spaniels, springers, a wirehaired fox terrier, two red dachshunds, Babs (the postmistress's old Pomeranian with bulging eyes), Donna's German shepherd and its pup, Ardella's black poodle, Tootie's three-legged Airedale that got caught in a trap set for wolves. Ranchers' dogs, too, will run with the river girls. No master's voice can hold them.

The girls take shortcuts down to the Clark Fork, to the Musselshell, to the Yellowstone, Flathead, Whitefish, Blackfoot, Stillwater, Tongue. Montana rivers belong to the river girls. They don't care what they have to do to claim them. They will rip fence posts straight out of the ground, hold the barbed strands flat so the yelping, galloping horde can jump over. Landowners shoot at them—rock salt, buckshot—but no one can hit them. River girls will do what they want to do. Not even their mothers can stop them.

Tootie and her bunch belong to the Flathead. They tear across fields that used to hold steers or alfalfa, now contain trailer-house occupants. They ride at full gallop over new-seeded lawns, topple tubs of petunias, scatter trailer-house cats and trailer-house children in their rush to get down to the river. A trailer-house woman shakes a fist at them. "I know where you're going, you bad, bad girls! I know what you're up to!" But river girls are already gone, down through the buck-brush and feathery grasses, down through the silver-dimed aspens, down to the willows that shelter them, to the cottonwood trees that love them.

Fishermen don't love them.

Fishing the Flathead, Dutch Anderson and his slow-witted son heard the yelps of the dogs, the whinny and splashing of horses. Dutch dropped his fish pole and tackle, turned for home, and ran. Ever slow, the boy waited on the riverbank, astonished in place, as the girls came swimming through the thick green shade. River girls speak softly of this, how the boy reached out to catch them, how he shouted a foul obscenity at them, how Ruth Ann on Dark Hunter scooped up river water and threw it at the boy's face. Dutch and his wife still search the river lands, looking for him. All they've ever found is a mountain ash twisted in the shape of a fisherman, fishline ingrown in the bark of its branches.

Ruth Ann isn't with them anymore. She became a cheerleader, and Joyce has heard that she's gone all the way with three different members of the Flathead Braves. (Ardella *will* not believe this. Delphina swears it is true!) Tootie will be the next to leave, though she would never say so. Her breasts have grown to the size of the small green apples on the tree by the homesteader's falling-down cabin. She's unbraided her hair and has combed it out in a kinky mass of marsh-gold or tansy. The last day of school, Pinky MacHarris asked if she'd go out with him when he got his new car, and she said no, not in ten million years.

She leads the way to the place they will go. She jumps the black Belgian from a white clay bank and into the river. The others follow. Smoothly as carousel horses, the sorrel, the pinto, the buckskin, the bay, go up and down, their legs reaching out underwater, drawing together, galloping underwater as they gallop on land, heads thrust out, ears forward, nostrils red with effort. The dogs form a V-shaped flotilla behind them: the Airedale, the spaniels, the brave little Pom— its fur fluffed out like a dandelion puff keeps it afloat. Sun slants across the surface of the water like fire, white fire, flaming around them, subliming them all into gold.

This is what they are up to:

They swim to an island in the middle of the Flathead. They will come ashore on gravel banks or sandbars, sand thick with river mint and hoptoads. And they will turn the horses inward, follow a streambed through wolf willow, wild blue iris, pink roses, through sumac implicit—poison or true. The mothering trees watch over them. They are going to the Place of the Dragon.

They tether their horses to thin green saplings, and they run through the river sand to the edge of the deep blue pool edged in snake-grass and water lilies. All together, the girls will jump in, climb out, jump in. They dive for gold flakes at the bottom of the pool, gold that will always avoid their grasp. Showers of gold rise up around them until they are swimming through clouds of shimmering gold, suspended in water as clear as the vapors of heaven. They weave garlands for their necks, they sing what river girls sing. And they talk, they talk about the time when they will have bosoms, and will walk like Madonna, and sleep in the arms of the boys from their school. But they *won't* have babies, on this they're agreed. No matter how the boys bug them, they won't give in.

Think how the forest has fallen to silence. The smallest of leaves will not tremble. Tootie is chosen this year, so she stands up, steps up to the edge of the pool. She dusts the sand off one shoulder and thigh, hipless, her long legs coltish and dancing. She glances back at the others, at the horses on their tethers, at the dogs beneath the trees, then she calls out across the pool and into the shadows of the cottonwood grove, and waits for the echoing answer.

"Dragon?"

...dragon, dragon, dragon...

"Are you home?"

...home, home, home...

The horses stand in the shade, hooves cocked, eyes closed. Even the dogs are quiet, hardly panting, hidden in the tall green grasses and rushes, waiting in the green leaves of willows.

"Tell me, Dragon, who will I love?"

...love, love, love...

Tootie gasps and covers her mouth with her hands.

Debbie whispers, "Don't be scared, go on, ask the question!"

Tootie calls out to the darkness moving through the trees. "Dragon, will anyone love me?"

...me, me, me...

"Dragon, will I marry?"

...marry, marry, marry...

At this, the girl falls over backward, laughing and laughing on the river sand. The river girls fall down beside her. They tease her and tickle her. They rub her breasts and her belly with willow leaves. They struggle to hold her, then let her go. She flees.

The girls chase after her, shrieking through the river brush, and the dogs jump up—the dachshunds, the Airedale, the German shepherd and its pup are barking and chasing her, too. The girls free the old Belgian from its tether, drop the halter rope, have to chase it through the undergrowth, weaving through the trees. They catch the old horse and lead him to the pool, lead him in. They climb on his back, bring him irises and roses to twine in his forelock and mane, white daisies for his tail, water lilies—both pink and white—and they want him to know how they love him, how they cherish him, how they're going to miss him, the big, black brute.

By the end of summer the Belgian will be put out to pasture, but only for the winter. He will always belong to the river girls—if not Tootie, to someone else, maybe Alice Starbuck, or Daphne Winters out on Fox Farm Road, maybe Kim or Cara will ride him next summer, maybe Starla.

Sometimes we see them on their run to the rivers, or watch them walk their horses across a high trestle—careful, setting each hoof down just so across the cross ties—or hear the yelping of the dogs late at night, sight the girls beneath the moon in autumn gardens, working their changes, doing what river girls do.

LATHER

Eros & Equus

See how the stallions shake
in every limb,
if they but catch the scent
of love upon the breeze.

—Virgil

From: JOY OF MAN'S DESIRING

Jean Giono

The stallion was like a light. The day shone through the oval window on his coat. Gradually one could distinguish the animal's contours. He was in a strongly braced stall, narrow at the sides and closed behind by two great tree trunks. He was a noble horse. His whole neck rose above the boards. He was sniffing at the hay rack. The soft part of his muzzle was extremely mobile. He was not eating. From time to time he would draw back his lip and with a corner of his tooth pull down two or three wisps of hay. He chewed. He whinnied with the sound of a woman weeping. He spat out the little green ball of grass. He stamped with his forefoot. He arched his neck two or three times. He shook his mane as if he were running in the open prairies. He quivered all over, and his strength flowed through his skin and muscles. He was stirred like the bed of a torrent that suddenly holds too much water. He kicked out with a great thrust of his hind hoofs. He struck with his shoes against the tree trunks. Very softly he whinnied again just for himself.

* * *

There were three animals lying in a dark litter of straw. Two were sleeping peacefully without any sound other than their breathing. They were geldings. One was sleeping, but she was softly neighing between her lips and quivering. It was a mare.

"She's dreaming," said Jacquou.

She had pink nostrils.

"She's like a stream," said Jacquou, "she moves from one end to the other. She is asleep but emotion is stirring her. Go open the door."

The great door, when opened, revealed the night toward the east, that is, in the opposite direction to the moon. The sky was terribly black and without depth, but the air was heavy with the odour of decaying leaves. One star, all by itself, very green and low on the horizon, was blowing a cold little north wind.

"Blackie!" called Jacquou. "Oh, black mare, wake up!"

She twitched her ears but did not open her eyes. She stretched, straightening her hind legs.

"Come on, old girl!"

He touched her. She did not wake up at once. She knew that is was not time for work and there was no reason for waking her. She thought that it was in her dream. But she smelt the odour of autumn, and the cold from the star that came in at the open door. She woke up and stood up at the same time.

"Let her alone," said Jacquou. "Oh, Blackie!"

She shook her head to find out whether she was still tied. She was no longer tied. She did not even have her halter on. She stretched her neck toward the door. She began to neigh a piercing little complaint. The other horses awoke. The sheep were trampling their beds. The sow grunted. The mare walked to the door. Her legs creaked. She continued to neigh and shake her head. When she reached the doorsill she stopped an instant. She was on the threshold, half in the night, half in the stable.

The farmhand raised the candle. They could see a kind of force swelling within the mare. At last, she darted out, first at a trot. After a moment they could hear her galloping.

It was dawn when Carle was awakened by the uproar that was shaking his stable. He was on his feet in an instant. He said: "What is that?" He looked around for his trousers, with his eyes not yet open. It sounded as if someone were demolishing the house with a sledge hammer.

The stallion was struggling against his chains, his side racks, his bars, and his bonds. Sparks flew beneath his iron shoes, the planks creaked, a cloud of dry hay dust filled the stable.

Carle tried to calm him with his usual words but he was forced to shout them with all his might, and that did not have the same effect. Carle danced about the maddened animal. He tried to put himself in front of the stallion's eyes.

"If he sees me," he thought, "perhaps he'll stop."

But this did not help. Fortunately, there was still the great girth under the animal's belly. Carle's son had come down too.

"Pull from your side!" shouted the father.

They both pulled on the ropes. The girth raised the struggling horse and he lost his footing. Immediately he grew still. He let his legs and neck hang. He was separated from the earth.

"What a business!" said Carle, wiping his brow.

Madame Carle had come to the door in her nightcap.

"Get out," said Carle, "sometimes the odour of a woman is enough."

"It isn't my odour," she said. "There is a mare outside. She is dancing in the pasture."

Carle opened the peep-hole in the folding door. In the light of dawn, a black mare was dancing in the middle of the pasture.

"It's Jacquou's Blackie!"

Then he remembered what he had said while they were cutting the rowen and he began to smile and raised his finger.

"Go into the kitchen," he said to Madame Carle. "I know what it's all about. You make some coffee. We're coming. You stay here son, you're going to see. Go along Philomène."

Then he said: "Shut the door to the corridor now, and open the big door."

The son opened the big door wide. The autumn dawn lighted a clear sky where blue and white were beginning to show.

"Get a stick," said Carle, "and make that little hussy dance a little further away. When she gets to the bottom of the pasture, you get out of the way."

He untied the stallion. He took everything off him. He took shelter behind the stall boards and eased the rope of the girth, first on one side, then on the other. The stallion touched ground once more. At the same time the girth fell off. For an instant the stallion stood motionless; then, head down, without looking where he was going, he bounded toward the open door.

Carle's son had taken refuge behind the fence. The black mare, driven to the far end of the pasture, was returning at a little trot. The stallion was galloping so hard toward her that he passed her. Then she wheeled about and followed him.

The nuptials of the horses lasted all day under a sky alive with a cavalcade of clouds and races of mingled shadow and sunshine. The

stallion bit the mare's nape. She hollowed her loins as if to spread and then she bounded away toward Randoulet's verdure. They galloped side by side, their manes smoking. The stallion kept trying to bite the warm, tingling spot behind the ears. The mare felt on her nape the stallion's saliva that grew cold in the wind made by their galloping. She longed for shade, grass, and peace. She galloped toward shade, grass, and peace. The stallion would pass her, then return to her. Their breasts crashed. They reared against each other. They beat the air with their forehoofs. They pressed their shod hoofs into their hair and the iron shoes slid in the sweat. They shook their heads, then fell to the ground and started off again at the same gallop. When they thus came to rear and clash, their male and female odours followed them a moment before dispersing in the cool wind.

Toward the middle of the morning they came to the great fields of grass that Randoulet had left standing. It was like an ocean of fresh hay, ripe beyond maturity, full of seeds, and on either side of the stem, two long tobacco-colored leaves that fell to dust at a touch. The field had no limit or end. Neither the stallion nor the mare knew grass growing wild. In spite of their great desire, they were both rooted by their four feet before this immense marvel. Their large eyes reflected the yellow of the grass. They could not eat because they had too great a longing for each other, but they sniffed in the odour for a long time. It was exactly what they both needed.

At an amble, they entered the thick grass. Gradually the hay rose to their breasts. The seed pods burst, the crushed dried leaves rose in blond dust.

At the end of Randoulet's pasture lay the pond, prostrate in its autumn sleep. It reflected the sky. It was like a hole in the earth through which the deep day could be seen. But before becoming empty and blue, with the reflection of birds and clouds, its shallow waters ran beneath the tall grasses mingled with rushes and reeds.

When the two animals reached it, they felt the coolness of the water rising up their legs. Their hoofs spread in the mud. They sniffed the odour of the pond. Their eyes were dazzled by the reflections in the water. They could hear the alarmed sharp snapping of the fins of big fishes. They began to dance up and down and the water splashed in long white arrows that sparkled in the sun as they shot above the grass. Then the coolness touched their bellies and their loins and their thighs, and it was already like the beginning of love. They felt the calming of the wildness of the passion which drew them toward each other. They rolled over in the water, crushing the grass and the edge of the pond and the mud. As the water bathed them they felt their wild passion change to tenderness, and when they rose again, a little stupefied, shivering, and covered with mud, they gently licked each other's nose, first around the mouth, then around the eyes.

Then, as they looked at the vast world about them, they perceived, far toward the north, the brown and green line of the forest. They circled the pond. After a long time they left the big pasture. They walked across country. They came to the forest. Almost all the trees had brown dead leaves. They sought the cool shade. An odour came from the east that told them that in that direction stood tall trees all green from root to tip.

They met a stag and some does and fawns. The stag fled at a bound; the does followed; the fawns bleated. The herd had left behind a strong odour of mating. The stallion put his head on the nape of the mare's neck. The mare stood still. The stallion did not bite. He began to walk on. The mare followed. He walked in front now, toward the green trees. At last he found them. They were almost at the edge of the forest. They were cedars. One in the middle was taller than the rest. It was very dark. It cast a black shadow. The stallion and the mare went toward the shadow that was shot with green rays. There they stopped. The stallion rested his heavy head on the mare's withers. She offered no resistance. The stallion remained a long time motionless, smelling the odour of female hair. Then, without raising his head, he gently approached the mare's great body that was trembling like a swarm of flies with quivers of desire. He licked her nape. He bent his head and gently nipped the mare's ears. She hollowed her back to open and stood waiting. Then he mounted her and made long and peaceful love.

Afterward they ate grass. They drank at the brook. They came out of the woods. The mare thought of the stable. She trotted quietly as if she were in harness. The stallion galloped beside her and around her. He would dance and go ten times as far as she in his gambollings. He cut off her path. She turned around him and continued to trot straight toward the stable. On the open plateau he succeeded in stopping her and making her submit once more for a long moment.

They were several hours wandering thus, then they came in sight of the stable. The roof rose above the earth. But they had made a wide detour toward the west and they came to the pastures where the white mare was. She bugled loudly and came and leaned against the fence. The stallion galloped toward her. The black mare took several steps in the direction of the stable, then resolutely stopped. She looked to see what the others were doing, then she began to eat.

The stallion tried to leap the fence; the white mare tried, too. At last, by pushing hard enough, they cracked the wood. Then the white mare rushed head on and split the fence. Carried onward by her momentum, she galloped over the fields. The stallion darted in pursuit. The black mare followed. Night was falling. All three horses disappeared at a gallop over the wide plateau. The stallion had already bitten the nape of the white mare's neck, and the traces of blood were visible on the white hair. The mare was laughing with open lips as she tossed her head.

RODEOIN'
THE REWARDS OF RODEO COWBOYS
Drum Hadley

As one of them rodeo cowboys said,
When he come a-blastin' out of the ropin' box,
At the rodeo grounds in Cheyenne, Wyoming,
Roped his calf, flung his slack, flew down the rope,
Tied that calf in twelve seconds flat,
Flung his hands up into the air…
"By God, I just knew the panties was a-gonna come,
Just a-sailin' into that arena."

—*Voice of an unknown rodeo cowboy*

From: LEGENDS OF THE FALL
Jim Harrison

Tristan had in his fever achieved that state which mystics crave but he was ill-prepared for: all things on earth both living and dead were with him and owned the same proportion, he did not recognize in any meaningful sense his naked foot at the end of the bed, or the ocean under whose lid it was always night even at high noon, the blood at the end of the great tusk did not belong on the schooner and throwing it overboard would somehow return it to the elephant's head. Susannah arrived as a pale pink sexual ghost and her womb covered him, saline like the spray off the bowspit until he was a ghost, too, and she was the ocean, Susannah herself, the bucking horse beneath him, the wood of the sea horse beneath him, both wind ripping the sails and the moon above the sails and the light of the dark between.

WHAT SHOCK HEARD

Pam Houston

It was late spring, but the dry winds had started already, and we were trying to load Shock into the horse trailer for a trip to the vet and the third set of X-rays on her fetlock. She's just barely green broke, and after months of being lame she was hot as a pistol and not willing to come within twenty yards of the trailer. Katie and Irwin, who own the barn, and know a lot more than me, had lip chains out, and lunge ropes and tranquilizer guns, but for all their contraptions they couldn't even get close enough to her to give her the shot. Crazy Billy was there too, screaming about two-by-fours and electric prods, and women being too damned ignorant to train a horse right. His horses would stand while he somersaulted in and out of the saddle. They'd stand where he ground-tied them, two feet from the train tracks, one foot off the highway. He

lost a horse under a semi once, and almost killed the driver. All the women were afraid of him, and the cowboys said he trained with Quaaludes. I was watching him close, trying to be patient with Katie and Irwin and my brat of a horse, but I didn't want Billy within ten feet of Shock, no matter how long it took to get her in the trailer.

That's when the new cowboy walked up, like out of nowhere with a carrot in his hands, whispered something in Shock's ear, and she walked right behind him into the trailer. He winked at me and I smiled back and poor Irwin and Katie were just standing there all tied up in their own whips and chains.

The cowboy walked on into the barn then, and I got into the truck with Katie and Irwin and didn't see him again for two months when Shock finally got sound and I was starting to ride her in short sessions and trying to teach her some of the things any five-year-old horse should know.

It was the middle of prairie summer by then and it was brutal just thinking about putting on long pants to ride, but I went off Shock so often I had to. The cowboy told me his name was Zeke, short for Ezekiel, and I asked him if he was religious and he said only about certain things.

I said my name was Raye, and he said that was his mother's name and her twin sister's name was Faye, and I said I could never understand why people did things like that to their children. I said that I was developing a theory that what people called you had everything to do with the person you turned out to become, and he said he doubted it 'cause that was just words, and was I going to stand there all day or was I going to come riding with him. He winked at Billy then and Billy grinned and I pretended not to see and hoped to myself that they weren't the same kind of asshole.

I knew Shock wasn't really up to the kind of riding I'd have to do to impress this cowboy, but it had been so long since I'd been out on the meadows I couldn't say no. There was something about the prairie for me—it wasn't where I had come from, but when I moved there it just took me in and I knew I couldn't ever stop living under that big sky. When I was a little girl driving with my family from our cabin in Montana across Nebraska to all the grandparents in Illinois, I used to be scared of the flatness because I didn't know what was holding all the air in.

Some people have such a fear of the prairie it makes them crazy, my ex-husband was one, and they even have a word for it: "agoraphobia." But when I looked it up in Greek it said "fear of the marketplace," and that seems like the opposite kind of fear to me. He was afraid of the high wind and the big storms that never even came while he was alive. When he shot himself, people said it was my fault for making him move here and making him stay, but his chart only said *acute agoraphobia* and I think he did it because his life wasn't as much like a book as he wanted it to be. He taught me about literature and language, and even though he used language in a bad way—to make up worlds that hurt us—I learned about its power and it got me a job, if nothing else, writing for enough money to pay off his debts.

But I wasn't thinking about any of that when I set off across the meadow at an easy hand gallop behind Zeke and his gelding Jesse. The sun was low in the sky, but it wasn't too long after solstice and in the summer the sun never seemed to fall, it seeped toward the horizon and then melted into it. The fields were losing heat, though, and at that pace we could feel the bands of warmth and cool coming out of the earth like it was some perfectly regulated machine. I could tell Zeke wasn't a talker, so I didn't bother riding up with him; I didn't want Shock to try and race on her leg. I hung back and watched the way his body moved with the big quarter horse: brown skin stretched across muscle and horseflesh, black mane and sandy hair, breath and sweat and one dust cloud rose around them till there was no way to separate the rider from the ride.

Zeke was a hunter. He made his living as a hunter's guide, in Alaska, in places so remote, he said, that the presence of one man with a gun was insignificant. He invited me home for moose steaks, and partly because I loved the way the two words sounded together, I accepted.

It was my first date in almost six years and once I got that into my head it wouldn't leave me alone. It had been almost two years since I'd been with a man, two years almost to the day that Charlie sat on our front-porch swing and blew his brains out with a gun so big the stains splattered three sets of windows and even wrapped around the corner of the house. I thought I had enough reason to swear off men for a

while, and Charlie wasn't in the ground three months when I got another one.

It was in October of that same year, already cold and getting dark too early, and Shock and I got back to the barn about an hour after sunset. Katie and Irwin were either in town or in bed and the barn was as dark as the house. I walked Shock into her stall and was starting to take off her saddle when Billy stepped out of the shadows with a shoeing tool in his hand. Women always say they know when it's going to happen, and I did, as soon as he slid the stall door open. I went down when the metal hit my shoulder and I couldn't see anything but I could feel his body shuddering already and little flecks of spit coming out of his mouth. The straw wasn't clean and Shock was nervous and I concentrated on the sound her hooves made as they snapped the air searching behind her. I imagined them connecting with Billy's skull and how the blood on the white wall would look like Charlie's, but Shock was much too honest a horse to aim for impact. Billy had the arm that wasn't numb pinned down with one knee through the whole thing, but I bit him once right on the jawline and he's still got that scar; a half-moon of my teeth in his face.

He said he'd kill me if I told, and the way my life was going it seemed reasonable to take him at his word. I had a hard time getting excited about meeting men after that. I'd learned to live without it, but not very well.

Shock had pitched me over her head twice that day that Zeke asked me to dinner, and by the time I got to his house my neck was so stiff I had to turn my whole body to look at him.

"Why don't you just jump in the hot tub before dinner," he said, and I swung my head and shoulders around from him to the wood-heated hot tub in the middle of the living room and I must have gone real white then because he said, "But you know, the heater's messing up and it's just not getting as hot as it should."

While he went outside to light the charcoals I sat on a hard wooden bench covered with skins facing what he called the trophy wall. A brown-and-white speckled owl stared down its pointed beak at me from above the doorway, its wings and talons poised as if ready for attack, a violence in its huge yellow eyes that is never so complete in humans.

He came back in and caught me staring into the face of the grizzly bear that covered most of the wall. "It's an eight-foot-square bear," he said, and then explained, by rubbing his hand across the fur, that it was eight feet long from the tip of its nose to the tip of its tail, and from the razor edge of one outstretched front claw to the other. He smoothed the fur back down with strong even strokes. He picked something off one of its teeth.

"It's a decent-sized bear," he said, "but they get much bigger."

I told him about the time I was walking with my dogs along the Salmon River and I saw a deer carcass lying in the middle of an active spawning ground. The salmon were deeper than the water and their tails slapped the surface as they clustered around the deer. One dog ran in to chase them, and they didn't even notice, they swam around her ankles till she got scared and came out.

He laughed and reached towards me and I thought *for* me, but then his hand came down on the neck of a six-point mule deer mounted on the wall behind me. "Isn't he beautiful?" he asked. His hands rubbed the short hair around the deer's ears. It was hanging closer to me than I realized, and when I touched its nose it was warmer than my hands.

He went back outside then and I tried to think of more stories to tell him but I got nervous all over and started fidgeting with something that I realized too late was the foot of a small furry animal. The thing I was sitting on reminded me a little too much of my dog to allow me to relax.

The moose steaks were lean and tender and it was easy to eat them until he started telling me about their history, about the bull that had come to the clearing for water, and had seen Zeke there, had seen the gun even, and trusted him not to fire. I couldn't look right at him then, and he waited awhile and he said, "Do you have any idea what they do to cows?"

We talked about other things after that, horses and the prairie and the mountains we had both left for it. At two I said I should go home, and he said he was too tired to take me. I wanted him to touch me the way he touched the mule deer but he threw a blanket over me and told me to lift up for the pillow. Then he climbed up and into a loft I hadn't even noticed, and left me down there in the dark under all those frightened eyes.

The most remarkable thing about him, I guess, was his calm: His hands were quieter on Jesse's mane even than mine were on Shock's. I never heard him raise his voice, even in laughter. There wasn't an animal in the barn he couldn't turn to putty, and I knew it must be the same with the ones he shot.

On our second ride he talked more, even about himself some, horses he'd sold, and ex-lovers; there was a darkness in him I couldn't locate.

It was the hottest day of that summer and it wouldn't have been right to run the horses, so we let them walk along the creek bank all afternoon, clear into the next county, I think.

He asked me why I didn't move to the city, why I hadn't, at least, while Charlie was sick, and I wondered what version of my life he had heard. I told him I needed the emptiness and the grasses and the storm threats. I told him about my job and the articles I was working on and how I knew if I moved to the city, or the ocean, or even back to the mountains, I'd be paralyzed. I told him that it seemed as if the right words could only come to me out of the perfect semicircular space of the prairie.

He rubbed his hands together fist to palm and smiled, and asked if I wanted to rest. He said he might nap, if it was quiet, and I said I knew I always talked too much, and he said it was okay because I didn't mind if he didn't always listen.

I told him words were all we had, something that Charlie had told me, and something I had believed because it let me fall into a vacuum where I didn't have to justify my life.

Zeke was stretching his neck in a funny way, so without asking I went over and gave him a back rub and when I was finished he said, "For a writer lady you do some pretty good communicating without words," but he didn't touch me even then, and I sat very still while the sun melted, embarrassed and afraid to even look at him.

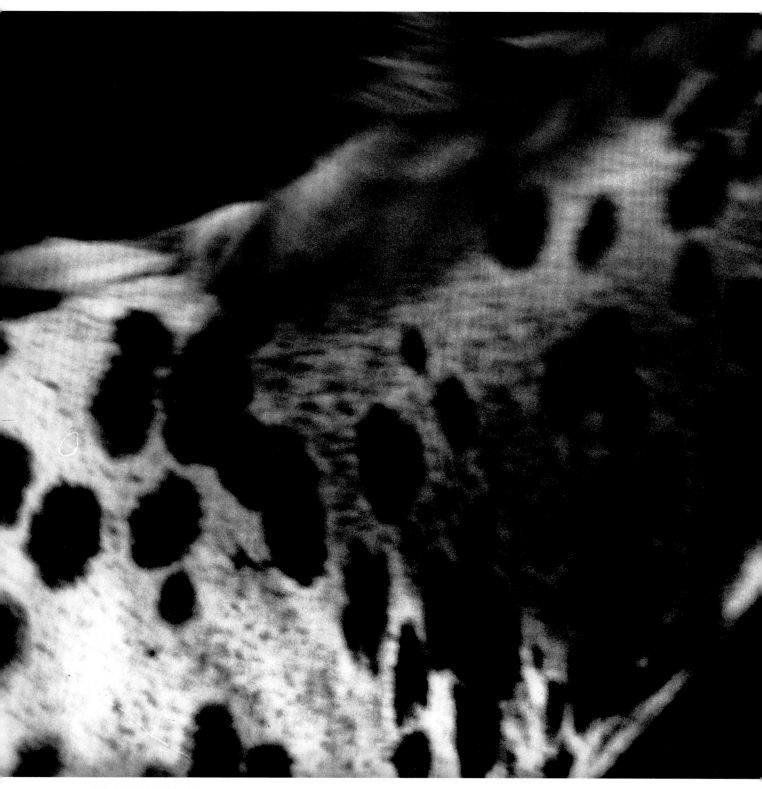

Finally, he stood up and stretched.

"Billy says you two go out sometimes."

"Billy lies," I said.

"He knows a lot about you," he said.

"No more than everyone else in town," I said. "People talk. It's just what they do. I'll tell you all about it if you want to know."

"We're a long way from the barn," he said, in a way that I couldn't tell if it was good or bad. He was rubbing one palm against the other so slowly it was making my skin crawl.

"Shock's got good night vision," I said, as evenly as I could.

He reached for a strand of Shock's mane and she rubbed her whole neck against him. I pulled her forelock out from under the brow band. She nosed his back pockets, where the carrots were. She knocked his cap off his head and scratched her nose between his shoulder blades. He put both hands up on her withers and rubbed little circles. She stretched her neck out long and low.

"Your horse is a whore, Raye," he said.

"I want to know what you said to her to make her follow you into the trailer," I said.

"What I said to her?" he said. "Christ, Raye, there aren't any words for that."

Then he was up and in the saddle and waiting for me to get back on Shock. He took off when I had only one foot in the stirrup, and I just hung around Shock's neck for the first quarter mile till he slowed up.

The creek trail was narrow and Shock wanted to race, so I got my stirrup and let her fly past him on the outside, the wheat so high it whipped across Shock's shoulder and my thigh. Once we were in the lead, Shock really turned it on and I could feel her strength and the give of her muscles and the solidity of the healed fetlock every time it hit the ground. Then I heard Jesse coming on the creek side, right at Shock's flank, and I knew we were coming to the big ditch, and I knew Shock would take it if Jesse did, but neither of us wanted to give up the lead. Shock hit the edge first and sailed over it and I came way up on her neck and held my breath when her front legs hit, but then we were down on the other side and she was just as strong and as sound as ever. Jesse edged up again and I knew we couldn't hold the lead for much longer. I felt

Zeke's boots on my calf and our stirrups locked once for an instant and then he pulled away. I let Shock slow then, and when Jesse's dust cleared, the darkening sky opened around me like an invitation.

It wasn't light enough to run anymore and we were still ten miles from the barn. Jupiter was up, and Mars. There wasn't any moon.

Zeke said, "Watching you ride made me almost forget to beat you." I couldn't see his face in the shadows.

He wanted silence but it was too dark not to talk, so I showed him the constellations. I told him the stories I knew about them: Cassiopeia weeping on the King's shoulder while the great winged Pegasus carries her daughter off across the eastern sky. Cygnus, the swan, flying south along the Milky Way, the Great Bear spinning slowly head over tail in the north. I showed him Andromeda, the galaxy closest to our own. I said, "It's two hundred million light-years away. Do you know what that means?" And when he didn't answer I said, "It means the light we see left that galaxy two hundred million years ago." And then I said, "Doesn't that make you feel insignificant?"

And he said, "No."

"How does it make you feel?" I said.

"Like I've gotten something I might not deserve," he said.

Then he went away hunting in Montana for six weeks. I kept thinking about him up there in the mountains I had come from and wondering if he saw them the way I did, if he saw how they held the air. He didn't write or call once, and I didn't either, because I thought I was being tested and I wanted to pass. He left me a key so I could water his plants and keep chemicals in his hot tub. I got friendly with the animals on the wall, and even talked to them sometimes, like I did to the plants. The only one I avoided was the Dall sheep. Perfect in its whiteness, and with a face as gentle and wise as Buddha. I didn't want to imagine Zeke's hands pulling the trigger that stained the white neck with blood the taxidermist must have struggled to remove.

He asked me to keep Jesse in shape for him too, and I did. I'd work Shock in the ring for an hour and then take Jesse out on the trails. He was a little nervous around me, being used to Zeke's uncanny calm, I guess, so I sang the songs to him that I remembered from Zeke's records: "Angel from Montgomery," "City of New Orleans," "L.A. Freeway," places I'd never been or cared to go. I didn't know any songs about Montana.

When we'd get back to the barn I'd brush Jesse till he shone, rubbing around his face and ears with a chamois cloth till he finally let down his guard a little and leaned into my hands. I fed him boxes full of carrots while Shock looked a question at me out of the corner of her eye.

One night Jesse and I got back late from a ride and the only car left at the barn was Billy's. I walked Jesse up and down the road twice before I thought to look in Zeke's saddlebags for the hunting knife I should have known would be there all along. I put it in the inside pocket of my jean jacket and felt powerful, even though I hadn't thought ahead as far as using it. When I walked through the barn door I hit the breaker switch that turned on every light and there was Billy leaning against the door to Jesse's stall.

"So now she's riding his horse," he said.

"You want to open that door?" I said. I stood as tall as I could between him and Jesse.

"Does that mean you're going steady?"

"Let me by," I said.

"It'd be a shame if he came back and there wasn't any horse to ride," he said, and I grabbed for Jesse's reins but he moved forward faster, spooking Jesse, who reared and spun and clattered out the open barn door. I listened to his hooves on the stone and then outside on the hard dirt till he got so far away I only imagined it.

Billy shoved me backwards into a wheelbarrow and when my head hit the manure I reached for the knife and got it between us and he took a step backwards and wiped the spit off his mouth.

"You weren't that much fun the first time," he said, and ran for the door. I heard him get into his car and screech out the driveway, and I lay there in the manure, breathing horse piss and praying he wouldn't hit Jesse out on the hard road. I got up slow and went into the tack room for a towel and I tried to clean my hair with it but it was Zeke's and it smelled like him and I couldn't understand why my timing had been so bad all my life. I wrapped my face in it so tight I could barely breathe and sat on his tack box and leaned into the wall, but then I remembered Jesse and put some grain in a bucket and went out into the darkness and whistled.

It was late September and almost midnight and all the stars I'd shown Zeke had shifted a half turn to the west. Orion was on the horizon, his bow drawn back, aimed across the Milky Way at the Great Bear, I guess, if space curves the way Earth does. Jesse wasn't anywhere, and I walked half the night looking for him. I went to sleep in my truck and at dawn Irwin and Jesse showed up at the barn door together.

"He got spooked," I told Irwin. "I was too worried to go home."
Irwin looked hard at me. "Hear anything from Zeke?" he said.

I spent a lot of time imagining his homecoming. I'd make up the kind of scenes in my head I knew would never happen, the kind that never happen to anyone, where the man gets out of the car so fast he tears his jacket, and when he lifts the woman up against the sky she is so light that she thinks she may be absorbed into the atmosphere.

I had just come back from a four-hour ride when his truck did pull up to the barn, six weeks to the day from when he left. He got out slow as ever, and then went around back to where he kept his carrots. From the tack-room window I watched him rub Jesse and feed him, pick up one of his front hooves, run his fingers through his tail.

I wanted to look busy but I'd just got done putting everything away so I sat on the floor and started oiling my tack and then wished I hadn't because of what I'd smell like when he saw me. It was fifteen minutes before he even came looking, and I had the bridle apart, giving it the oil job of its life. He put his hands on the doorjamb and smiled big.

"Put that thing back together and come riding with me," he said.
"I just got back," I said. "Jesse and I've been all over."
"That'll make it easier for you to beat me on your horse," he said. "Come on, it's getting dark earlier every night."
He stepped over me and pulled his saddle off the rack, and I put the bridle back together as fast as I could. He was still ready before I was and he stood real close while I tried to make Shock behave and get tacked up and tried not to let my hands shake when I fastened the buckles.

Then we were out in the late sunshine and it was like he'd never left, except this time he was galloping before he hit the end of the driveway.

"Let's see that horse run," he called to me, and Jesse shot across the road and the creek trail and plunged right through the middle of the wheat field. The wheat was so tall I could barely see Zeke's head, but the footing was good and Shock was gaining on him. I thought about the farmer who'd shoot us if he saw us, and I thought about all the hours I'd spent on Jesse keeping him in shape so that Zeke could come home and win another race. The sky was black to the west and coming in fast, and I tried to remember if I'd heard a forecast and to feel if there was any direction to the wind. Then we were out in a hay field that had just been cut and rolled, and it smelled so strong and sweet it made me light-headed and I thought maybe we weren't touching ground at all but flying along above it, buoyed up by the fragrance and the swirl of the wind. I drove Shock straight at a couple of bales that were tied together and made her take them, and she did, but by the time we hit the irrigation ditch we'd lost another couple of seconds on Zeke.

I felt the first drops of rain and tried to yell up to Zeke, but the wind came up suddenly and blasted my voice back into my mouth. I knew there was no chance of catching him then, but I dug my heels in and yipped a little and Shock dug in even harder, but then I felt her front hoof hit a gopher hole and the bottom dropped out and she went down and I went forward over her neck and then she came down over me. My face hit first and I tasted blood and a hoof came down on the back of my head and I heard the reins snap and waited for another hoof to hit, but then it was quiet and I knew she had cleared me. At least I'm not dead, I thought, but my head hurt too bad to even move.

I felt the grit inside my mouth and thought of Zeke galloping on across the prairie, enclosed in the motion, oblivious to my fall. It would be a mile, maybe two, before he slowed down and looked behind him, another before he'd stop, aware of my absence, and come back for me.

I opened one eye and saw Shock grazing nearby, broken reins hanging uneven below her belly. If she'd re-pulled the tendon in her fetlock it would be weeks, maybe months, before I could ride with him again. My mouth was full of blood and my lips were swelling so much it was running out the sides, though I kept my jaw clamped and my head down. The wind was coming in little gusts now, interrupted by longer and longer periods of calm, but the sky was getting darker and I lifted my head to look for Zeke. I got dizzy, and I closed my eyes and tried to breathe regularly. In what seemed like a long time I started to hear a rhythm in my head and I pressed my ear into the dust and knew it was Zeke coming back across the field at a gallop, balanced and steady, around the holes and even over them. Then I heard his boots hit ground. He tied Jesse first, and then caught Shock, which was smart, I guess, and then he knelt next to my head and I opened the eye that wasn't in the dirt and he smiled and put his hands on his knees.

"Your mouth," he said, without laughing, but I knew what I must've looked like, so I raised up on one elbow and started to tell him I was okay and he said,

"Don't talk. It'll hurt."

And he was right, it did, but I kept on talking and soon I was telling him about the pain in my mouth and the back of my head and what Billy had done that day in the barn, and the ghosts I carry with me. Blood was coming out with the words and pieces of tooth, and I kept talking till I told him everything, but when I looked at his face I knew all I'd done was make the gap wider with the words I'd picked so carefully that he didn't want to hear. The wind started up again and the rain was getting steady.

I was crying then, but not hard, and you couldn't tell through all the dirt and blood, and the rain and the noise the wind was making. I was crying, I think, but I wanted to laugh because he would have said there weren't any words for what I didn't tell him, and that was that I loved him and even more I loved the prairie that wouldn't let you hide anything, even if you wanted to.

Then he reached across the space my words had made around me and put his long brown finger against my swollen lips. I closed my eyes tight as his hand wrapped up my jaw and I fell into his chest and whatever it was that drove him to me, and I held myself there unbreathing, like waiting for the sound of hooves on the sand, like waiting for a tornado.

SLEEPING WITH HORSES
Lyn Lifshin

though I never have, I dream
of such warm flanks,
pulse of blood deep
enough to blur night
terror. I want my own
mare, sleek, night
colored to block
memories of the
orchard of bones,
the loved-lost under
leaves, under a quilt
of guilt. I think of
cats, long slept with
then gone, how
the Egyptians buried
not only wives but
their favorite pets
near them to cushion
their trip to the
underworld. I want
this mare, velvety
as the dream mare's
nose, nuzzling my
skin in the black
that braids us into
one so I won't
move unless she does

From: MY HORSES, MY TEACHERS

Alois Podhajsky

Observing closely the relationship of horses we will discover that they, too, may have sympathies or unfriendly feelings towards each other. Some will become such close friends that they grow restless if the partner has been taken away and will greet him with expressions of pleasure when he returns. My brave Neapolitano Africa was used to having his box next to that of Teja and especially on our trips to London and St. Gallen, Switzerland, the two horses were inseparable comrades. In the vast stables of White City in London, some hundred horses were housed in boxes and stalls but Neapolitano Africa did not pay the slightest attention even to the mares around him. While Teja was away performing or being trained he waited impatiently for him and grew quiet only when his friend was again safely in the neighbouring box.

It is not rare at all to find among horses this feeling that they belong together. The old head riders told me that on the occasion of the trips to Germany that the Spanish Riding School had undertaken in 1925 the Lipizzaners had displayed great dignity and the obvious pride in their breed. In the midst of the other horses at the show they paid attention only to their brothers and did not miss an opportunity to watch them at work. Later I had occasion to obtain proof that these old masters had not told me any fantastic stories but that this was really true. I myself have seen that when the Lipizzaner stallions gave a display within a horse show they did not pay the slightest attention to any of the other horses around them or to the bustle of the show but stared intently in the direction where their comrades performed. It made me think of a theatre when some actors remain hidden in the wings to watch the stars of the group. It struck me especially on these tours of the Spanish Riding School that even stallions who had been to the stud farm for several terms never deigned to look at other horses although there were mares among them. Not even the different colour of the mares aroused any interest although on other occasions the white stallions had manifested a preference for horses of different colouring.

To what problem this predilection might lead was demonstrated by the stallion Siglavy Neapolitano—for some it was not the name of the dam that was used in these double names but that of her sire. Siglavy Neapolitano was not at all inclined to favour the white Lipizzaner mares. He was simply not interested in them while he was strongly attracted by the brown Nonius mares that were used on the same farm for a half-breed strain. The director of the stud farm tried every conceivable method to put the stallion into a kind disposition because it was very important to produce foals of the Siglavy line, which was represented by only a few horses at that time. The white Lipizzaner mare was even dyed with calcium permanganicum, a method by which grey horses in the Army were made less visible from a distance during the First World War. But it did not help either, for the clever stallion was not to be taken in by a swindle and his aversion to the Lipizzaner mares manifested itself even more strongly. There was no use playing tricks on him. The director of the stud farm was in despair until he had yet another idea. He chose a young and lovely Nonius mare in season and had her walk up and down in front of the reluctant Lipizzaner stallion. Immediately he expressed the greatest interest and because she remained forever inaccessible his desire grew to such an extent that in the end he resigned and put up with the ersatz of his Lipizzaner bride who had originally been chosen for him. What a strange role for the poor Nonius mare to earn her oats as a "come-on"!

From: CHU CHU

Bret Harte

I do not believe that the most enthusiastic lover of that "useful and noble animal," the horse, will claim for him the charm of geniality, humor, or expansive confidence. Any creature who will not look you squarely in the eye—whose only oblique glances are inspired by fear, distrust, or a view to attack; who has no way of returning caresses, and whose favorite expression is one of head-lifting disdain, may be "noble" or "useful," but can be hardly said to add to the gaiety of nations. Indeed it may be broadly stated that, with the single exception of goldfish, of all animals kept for the recreation of mankind the horse is alone capable of exciting a passion that shall be absolutely hopeless. I deem these general remarks necessary to prove that my unreciprocated affection for Chu Chu was not purely individual or singular. And I may add that to these general characteristics she brought the waywardness of her capricious sex.

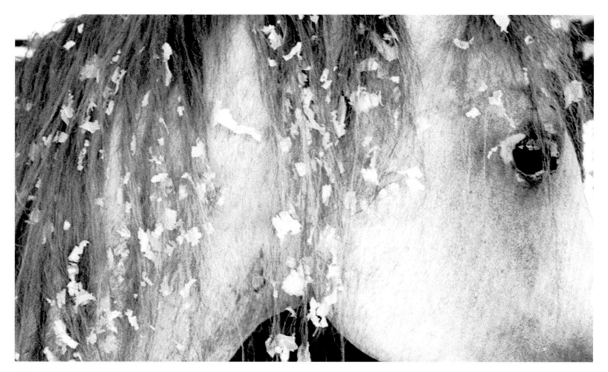

She came to me out of the rolling dust of an emigrant wagon, behind whose tailboard she was gravely trotting. She was a half-broken filly—in which character she had at different times unseated everybody in the train—and, although covered with dust, she had a beautiful coat, and the most lambent gazelle-like eyes I had ever seen. I think she kept those latter organs purely for ornament—apparently looking at things with her nose, her sensitive ears, and, sometimes, even a slight lifting of her slim near foreleg. On our first interview I thought she favored me with a coy glance, but as it was accompanied by an irrelevant "Look out!" from her owner, the teamster, I was not certain. I only know that after some conversation, a good deal of mental reservation, and the disbursement of considerable coin, I found myself standing in the dust of the departing emigrant wagon with one end of a forty-foot riata in my hand, and Chu Chu at the other.

I pulled invitingly at my own end, and even advanced a step or two toward her. She then broke into a long disdainful pace, and began to circle round me at the extreme limit of her tether. I stood admiring her free action for some moments—not always turning with her, which was tiring—until I found that she was gradually winding herself up *on me!* Her frantic astonishment when she suddenly found herself thus brought up against me was one of the most remarkable things I ever saw, and nearly took me off my legs. Then, when she had pulled against the riata until her narrow head and prettily arched neck were on a perfectly straight line with it, she as suddenly slackened the tension and condescended to follow me, at an angle of her own choosing. Sometimes it was on one side of me, sometimes on the other. Even then the sense of my dreadful contiguity apparently would come upon her like a fresh discovery, and she would become hysterical. But I do not think that she really *saw* me. She looked at the riata and sniffed it disparagingly; she pawed some pebbles that were near me tentatively with her small hoof; she started back with a Robinson Crusoe-like horror of my footprints in the wet gully, but my actual personal presence she ignored. She would sometimes pause, with her head thoughtfully between her forelegs, and apparently say: "There is some extraordinary presence here: animal, vegetable, or mineral—I can't make out which—but it's not good to eat, and I loath and detest it."

From: A HERO OF OUR TIME

Mikhail Lermontov

"That's a splendid horse of yours," Azamat was saying. "If I were master of a house of my own and had a stud of three hundred mares, I would give half of it for your galloper, Kazbich!'

"'Aha! Kazbich!' I said to myself, and I called to mind the coat of mail.

"'Yes,' replied Kazbich, after an interval of silence. 'There is not such another to be found in all Kabardia. Once—it was on the other side of the Terek—I had ridden with the Abreks to seize the Russian herds. We had no luck, so we scattered in different directions. Four Cossacks dashed after me. I could actually hear the cries of the giaours behind me, and in front of me there was a dense forest. I crouched down in the saddle, committed myself to Allah, and, for the first time in my life, insulted my horse with a blow of the whip. Like a bird, he plunged among the branches; the sharp thorns tore my clothing, the dead boughs of the cork-elms struck against my face! My horse leaped over tree trunks and burst his way through bushes with his chest! It would have been better for me to have abandoned him at the outskirts of the forest and concealed myself in it afoot, but it was a pity to part with him—and the Prophet rewarded me. A few bullets whistled over my head. I could now hear the Cossacks, who had dismounted, running upon my tracks. Suddenly a deep gully opened before me. My galloper took thought—and leaped. His hind hoofs slipped back off the opposite bank, and he remained hanging by his forefeet. I dropped the bridle and threw myself into the hollow, thereby saving my horse, which jumped out. The Cossacks saw the whole scene, only not one of them got down to search for me, thinking probably that I had mortally injured myself; and I heard them rushing to catch my horse. My heart bled within me. I crept along the hollow through the thick grass—then I looked around: it was the end of the forest. A few Cossacks were riding out from it on to the clearing, and there was my Karagyoz galloping straight towards them. With a shout they all dashed forward. For a long, long time they pursued him, and one of them, in particular, was once or twice almost successful in throwing a lasso over his neck.

I trembled, dropped my eyes, and began to pray. After a few moments I looked up again, and there was my Karagyoz flying along, his tail waving—free as the wind; and the giaours, on their jaded horses, were trailing along far behind, one after another, across the steppe. Wallah! It is true—really true! Till late at night I lay in the hollow. Suddenly—what do you think, Azamat? I heard in the darkness a horse trotting along the bank of the hollow, snorting, neighing, and beating the ground with his hoofs. I recognised my Karagyoz's voice; 'twas he, my comrade!'…Since that time we have never been parted!'

"And I could hear him patting his galloper's sleek neck with his hand, as he called him various fond names.

"'If I had a stud of a thousand mares,' said Azamat, 'I would give it all for your Karagyoz!'

"'Yok! I would not take it!' said Kazbich indifferently.

"'Listen, Kazbich,' said Azamat, trying to ingratiate himself with him. 'You are a kindhearted man, you are a brave horseman, but my father is afraid of the Russians and will not allow me to go on the mountains. Give me your horse, and I will do anything you wish. I will steal my father's best rifle for you, or his sabre—just as you like—and his sabre is a genuine Gurda; you have only to lay the edge against your hand, and it will cut you; a coat of mail like yours is nothing against it.'

"Kazbich remained silent.

"'The first time I saw your horse,' continued Azamat, 'when he was wheeling and leaping under you, his nostrils distended, and the flints flying in showers from under his hoofs, something I could not understand took place within my soul; and since that time I have been weary of everything. I have looked with disdain on my father's best gallopers; I have been ashamed to be seen on them, and yearning has taken possession of me. In my anguish I have spent whole days on the cliffs, and, every minute, my thoughts have kept turning to your black galloper with his graceful gait and his sleek back, straight as an arrow. With his keen, bright eyes he has looked into mine as if about to speak!… I shall die, Kazbich, if you will not sell him to me!" said Azamat, with trembling voice.

'I could hear him burst out weeping, and I must tell you that Azamat was a very stubborn lad, and that not for anything could tears be wrung from him, even when he was a little younger.

"In answer to his tears, I could hear something like a laugh.

"'Listen,' said Azamat in a firm voice. 'You see, I am making up my mind for anything. If you like, I will steal my sister for you! How she dances! How she sings! And the way she embroiders with gold—marvellous! Not even a Turkish Padishah has had a wife like her!… Shall I? Wait for me tomorrow night, yonder, in the gorge where the torrent flows; I will go by with her to the neighbouring village—and she is yours. Surely Bela is worth your galloper!'

"Kazbich remained silent for a long, long time. At length, instead of answering, he struck up in an undertone the ancient song:

"Many a beauty among us dwells
From whose eyes' dark depths the starlight wells,
'Tis an envied lot and sweet, to hold
Their love; but brighter is freedom bold.
Four wives are yours if you pay the gold;
But a mettlesome steed is of price untold;
The whirlwind itself on the steppe is less fleet;
He knows no treachery—no deceit."

"In vain Azamat entreated him to consent. He wept, coaxed, and swore to him. Finally, Kazbich interrupted him impatiently:

"'Begone, you crazy brat! How should you think to ride on my horse? In three steps you would be thrown and your neck broken on the stones!'

"'I?' cried Azamat in a fury, and the blade of the child's dagger rang against the coat of mail. A powerful arm thrust him away, and he struck the wattle fence with such violence that it rocked.

"'Now we'll see some fun!' I thought to myself.

From: LIKE WATER FOR CHOCOLATE

Laura Esquivel

On her the food seemed to act as an aphrodisiac; she began to feel an intense heat pulsing through her limbs. An itch in the center of her body kept her from sitting properly in her chair. She began to sweat, imagining herself on horseback with her arms clasped around one of Pancho Villa's men: the one she had seen in the village plaza the week before, smelling of sweat and mud, of dawns that brought uncertainty and danger, smelling of life and of death. She was on her way to market in Piedras Negras with Chencha, the servant, when she saw him coming down the main street, riding in front of the others, obviously the captain of the troop. Their eyes met and what she saw in his made her tremble. She saw all the nights he'd spent staring into the fire and longing to have a woman beside him, a woman like her. She got out her handkerchief and tried to wipe those sinful thoughts from her mind as she wiped away the sweat.

But it was no use, something strange had happened to her. She turned to Tita for help, but Tita wasn't there, even though her body was sitting up quite properly in her chair; there wasn't the slightest sign of life in her eyes. It was as if a strange alchemical process had dissolved her entire being in the rose petal sauce, in the tender flesh of her quails, in the wine, in every one of the meal's aromas. That was the way she entered Pedro's body, hot, voluptuous, perfumed, totally sensuous.

With that meal it seemed they had discovered a new system of communication, in which Tita was the transmitter, Pedro the receiver, and poor Gertrudis the medium, the conducting body through which the singular sexual message was passed.

Pedro didn't offer any resistance. He let Tita penetrate to the farthest corners of his being, and all the while they couldn't take their eyes off each other. He said:

"Thank you, I have never had anything so exquisite."

It truly is a delicious dish. The roses give it an extremely delicate flavor.

After the petals are removed from the roses, they are ground with the anise in a mortar. Separately, brown the chestnuts in a pan, remove the peels, and cook them in water. Then, puree them. Mince the garlic and brown slightly in butter; when it is transparent, add it to the chestnut puree, along with the honey, the ground pitaya, and the rose petals, and salt to taste. To thicken the sauce slightly, you may add two teaspoons of cornstarch. Last, strain through a fine sieve and add no more than two drops of attar of roses, since otherwise it might have too strong a flavor and smell. As soon as the seasoning has been added, remove the sauce from the heat. The quail should be immersed in this sauce for ten minutes to infuse them with the flavor, and then removed.

The smell of attar of roses is so penetrating that the mortar used to grind the petals will smell like roses for several days.

The job of washing that and all the other kitchen utensils fell to Gertrudis. She washed them after each meal, out on the patio, so she could throw the scraps left in the pans to the animals. Since some of the utensils were large, it was also easier to wash them in the wash basin. But the day they had the quail, she asked Tita to do the washing up for her. Gertrudis was really stricken; her whole body was dripping with sweat. Her sweat was pink, and it smelled like roses, a lovely strong smell. In desperate need of a shower, she ran to get it ready.

Behind the patio by the stable and the corn crib, Mama Elena had had a primitive shower rigged up. It was a small room made of planks nailed together, except that between one board and the next, there were such big cracks that it was easy to see the person who was taking the shower. Still, it was the first shower of any kind that had ever been seen in the village. A cousin of Mama Elena's who lived in San Antonio, Texas, had invented it. It had a thirty-gallon tank that was six feet high: first, you filled the tank with water, then you got a shower using gravity. It was hard work carrying buckets of water up the wooden ladder, but it was delightful afterward just to open the tap and feel the water run over your whole body in a steady stream, not doled out the way it was if you bathed using gourds full of water. Years later some gringos got this invention from Mama Elena's cousin for a song and made a few improvements. They made thousands of showers that used pipes, so you didn't have to do all that damn filling.

If Gertrudis had only known! The poor thing climbed up and down ten times, carrying buckets of water. It was brutal exercise, which made the heat that burned her body grow more and more intense, until she nearly fainted.

The only thing that kept her going was the image of the refreshing shower ahead of her, but unfortunately she was never able to enjoy it, because the drops that fell from the shower never made it to her body: they evaporated before they reached her. Her body was giving off so much heat that the wooden walls began to split and burst into flame. Terrified, she thought she would be burnt to death, and she ran out of the little enclosure just as she was, completely naked.

By then the scent of roses given off by her body had traveled a long, long way. All the way to town, where the rebel forces and the federal troops were engaged in a fierce battle. One man stood head and shoulders above the others for his valor; it was the rebel who Gertrudis had seen in the plaza in Piedras Negras the week before.

A pink cloud floated toward him, wrapped itself around him, and made him set out at a gallop toward Mama Elena's ranch. Juan—for that was the soldier's name—abandoned the field of battle, leaving an enemy soldier not quite dead, without knowing why he did so. A higher power was controlling his actions. He was moved by a powerful urge to arrive as quickly as possible at a meeting with someone unknown in some undetermined place. But it wasn't hard to find. The aroma from Gertrudis' body guided him. He got there just in time to find her racing through the field. Then he knew why he'd been drawn there. This woman desperately needed a man to quench the red-hot fire that was raging inside her.

A man equal to loving someone who needed love as much as she did, a man like him.

Gertrudis stopped running when she saw him riding toward her. Naked as she was, with her loosened hair falling to her waist, luminous, glowing with energy, she might have been an angel and devil in one woman. The delicacy of her face, the perfection of her pure virginal body contrasted with the passion, the lust, that leapt from her eyes, from her every pore. These things, and the sexual desire Juan had contained for so long while he was fighting in the mountains, made for a spectacular encounter.

Without slowing his gallop, so as not to waste a moment, he leaned over, put his arm around her waist, and lifted her onto the horse in front of him, face to face, and carried her away. The horse, which seemed to be obeying higher orders too, kept galloping as if it already knew their ultimate destination, even though Juan had thrown the reins aside and was passionately kissing and embracing Gertrudis. The movement of the horse combined with the movement of their bodies as they made love for the first time, at a gallop and with a great deal of difficulty.

They were going so fast that the escort following Juan never caught up with him. Liars tell half-truths and he told everyone that during the battle the captain had suddenly gone crazy and deserted the army.

That is the way history gets written, distorted by eyewitness accounts that don't really match the reality. Tita saw the incident from a completely different perspective than the rebel soldiers. She watched the whole thing from the patio as she was washing the dishes. She didn't miss a thing in spite of the rosy clouds of steam and the flames shooting out of the bathroom, which made it hard for her to see. Pedro, too, was lucky enough to witness the spectacle, since he was just leaving the patio on his bicycle to go for a ride.

Like silent spectators to a movie, Pedro and Tita began to cry watching the stars act out the love that was denied to them. There was a moment, one brief instant, when Pedro could have changed the course of their story. Taking Tita's hand in his, he began to talk to her: —Tita… But that was all. There was no time to finish. He was forced back to grim reality. He had heard Mama Elena's shout, asking what was going on out on the patio. If Pedro had asked Tita to run away with him, she wouldn't have hesitated for a moment, but he didn't; instead, he quickly hopped onto his bicycle and furiously pedaled away.

From: ST. MAWR

D.H. Lawrence

"May I say *how do you do?*" she said to the horse, drawing a little nearer in her white, summery dress, and lifting her hand that glittered with emeralds and diamonds.

He drifted away from her, as if some wind blew him. Then he ducked his head, and looked sideways at her, from his black, full eye.

"I think I'm all right," she said, edging nearer, while he watched her.

She laid her hand on his side, and gently stroked him. Then she stroked his shoulder, and then the hard, tense arch of his neck. And she was startled to feel the vivid heat of his life come through to her, through the lacquer of red-gold gloss. So slippery with vivid, hot life!

She paused, as if thinking, while her hand rested on the horse's sun-arched neck. Dimly, in her weary young-woman's soul, an ancient understanding seemed to flood in.

She wanted to buy St. Mawr.

"I think," she said to Saintsbury, "if I can, I will buy him."

The man looked at her long and shrewdly.

"Well, my Lady," he said at last, "there shall be nothing kept from you. But what would your Ladyship do with him, if I may make so bold?"

"I don't know," she replied, vaguely. "I might take him to America."

The man paused once more then said:

"They say it's been the making of some horses, to take them over the water, to Australia or such places. It might repay you—you never know."

She wanted to buy St. Mawr. She wanted him to belong to her. For some reason the sight of him, his power, his alive, alert intensity, his unyieldingness, made her want to cry.

She never did cry: except sometimes with vexation, or to get her own way. As far as weeping went, her heart felt as dry as a Christmas walnut. What was the good of tears, anyhow? You had to keep on holding on, in this life, never give way, and never give in. Tears only left one weakened and ragged.

But now, as if that mysterious fire of the horse's body had split some rock in her, she went home and hid herself in her room, and just cried. The wild, brilliant, alert head of St. Mawr seemed to look at her out of another world. It was as if she had had a vision, as if the walls of her own world had suddenly melted away, leaving her in a great darkness, in the midst of which the large, brilliant eyes of that horse looked at her with demonish question, while his naked ears stood up like daggers from the naked lines of his inhuman head, and his great body glowed red with power.

What was it? Almost like a god looking at her terribly out of the everlasting dark, she had felt the eyes of that horse; great, glowing, fearsome eyes, arched with a question, and containing a white blade of light like a threat. What was his non-human question, and his uncanny threat? She didn't know. He was some splendid demon, and she must worship him.

From: FREE REIN

Laura Chester

The profound blankness of a deep trance, the crystal's coma
would now be nice, as the needle, drill and scalpel scrape—
she pictures the power, *unleashed*, through her own gloved hands,
the stallion allowed to work and *breathe* up on the top in large
green circles, fields alone, the wind released—just to imagine
that acceleration, the subtle pressure, leather, response, and liking that,
just right between, while the others walked, and knew not. She rode—
flew over pain all bruised and roses swollen, to loosen the bands that
clench the teeth, calming down with talk and pat, to await the golden
awaited day, when the face is freed like the moon floats over the fields
and rounds of hay, the memory filled with the smell of leaves pressed
dark with damp and corn fermenting, trees raked, and the air reborn,
renata to you, who never was even half-afraid by the boot caught trapped
in the steel stirrup, the power of all unspoken words, while sighting that
trail of glittering sequence, that leads, when followed, to dangerous
knowledge.

From: EQUUS

Peter Shaffer

I was pushed forward on the horse. There was sweat on my legs from his neck. The fellow held me tight, and let me turn the horse which way I wanted. All that power going any way you wanted… His sides were all warm, and the smell… Then suddenly I was on the ground, where Dad pulled me. I could have bashed him…

Pause.

Something else. When the horse first appeared, I looked up into his mouth. It was huge. There was this chain in it. The fellow pulled it, and cream dripped out. I said 'Does it hurt?' And he said—the horse said—said—

He stops, in anguish. Dysart makes a note in his file.

[*desperately*] It was always the same, after that. Every time I heard one clop by, I had to run and see. Up a country lane or anywhere. They sort of pulled me. I couldn't take my eyes off them. Just to watch their skins. The way their necks twist, and sweat shines in the folds… [*pause*] I can't remember when it started. Mum reading to me about Prince who no one could ride, except one boy. Or the white horse in Revelations. 'He that sat upon him was called Faithful and True. His eyes were flames of fire, and he had a name written that no man knew but himself'… Words like reins. Stirrup, Flanks… 'Dashing his spurs against his charger's flanks!'… Even the words made me feel—…Years, I never told anyone. Mum wouldn't understand. She likes Equitation'. Bowler hats and jodhpurs! 'My grandfather dressed for the horse,' she says. What does that mean? The horse isn't dressed. It's the most naked thing you ever saw! More than a dog or a cat or anything. Even the most broken down old nag has got its *life!* To put a bowler on it is *filthy!*… Putting them through their paces! Bloody gymkhanas!… No one understands!… Except cowboys. They do. I wish I was a cowboy. They're free. They just swing up and then it's miles of grass… I bet all cowboys are *orphans!*… I bet they are!

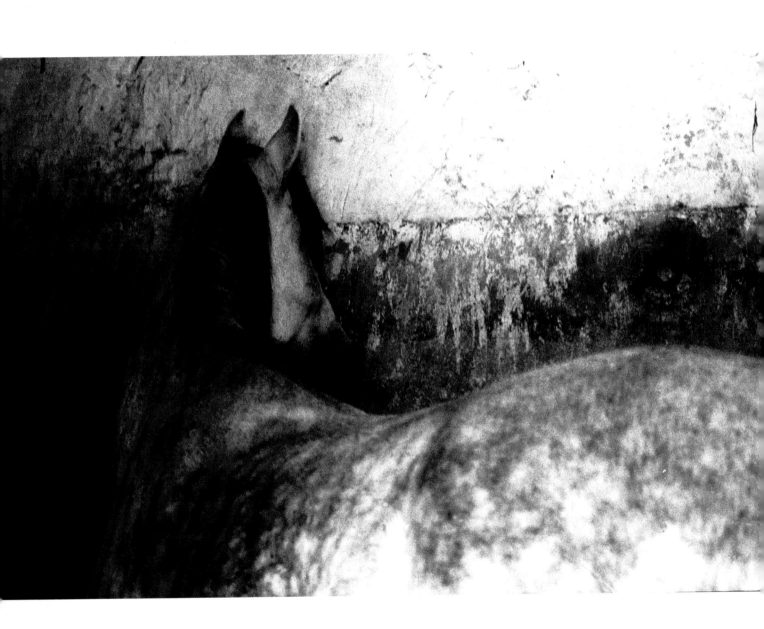

From: SHE FLIES WITHOUT WINGS
Mary Midkiff

*Th*e stallion was my responsibility for about half a year. During that time, my periods began. Every time I cycled, the stallion announced my hormonal state to the world by his agitated reaction to my presence. Eventually others noticed the horse's flirtation. The farm master told me to smack the stud and give him a firm "No!" when he began showing his admiration, but I rarely did. The presence and effect of pheromones was something they hadn't taught in health class at school; the horse's uninhibited response gave me an insight into what was going on inside those boys I watched from a curious distance within my own herd.

My barn admirer always remained under control and I never felt threatened or endangered by him. Over time I began to see some humor in the situation. When I groomed him, he would nicker softly, telling me how much he enjoyed my touch. I found myself giggling over my brushes and wondering whether I would ever evoke the same undisguised pleasure in a boy—stallion of my own kind or whether I would experience it myself. In the presence of the randy horse, it became possible to imagine both possibilities. Horses had piqued my senses from earliest childhood; now, on the brink of womanhood, this one was indicating the road where the merely sensory evolved into something new and far more powerful.

At eighteen, I began working the Keeneland and Fasig-Tipton yearling sales, where some of the best and most promising Thoroughbreds are auctioned every season to buyers who gathered from all over the world. My job was to prepare and show yearlings in order to garner the best price in the sales ring. I normally met the youngsters a few months prior to the sales, when I began conditioning them as athletes through lengthy walks on a long lead line and teaching them manners in the barn and in the open. My first task was to gain their trust and train them to work with me as a partner when they were taken away from their pals—a bond that would

keep them focused in the presence of thousands of noisy people. If I performed my job well, the yearling finding himself in this stressful situation would look to me as his alpha mare for security and direction. He would do his best to stand quietly and calmly at my request and to present himself as a well-mannered, good-looking prospect worthy of much more attention than his cohorts who showed up disheveled and unruly.

For weeks before the sale, I rubbed the horses' coats to a smooth, slick finish, pulled their manes to a perfect length that accentuated their long neck muscles, moisturized each strand of their tails to hang down evenly and move gracefully with their walk. I trimmed ears, muzzle, and fetlocks; oiled hooves to the high gleam of a pair of new spats. Every preparation was both a means and an end: a means to fetching top dollar but also a satisfying indulgence in sensory pleasure for both me and the young animals.

July evenings in Kentucky are notoriously hot and sticky. The auction pavilion steams with perspiration and cigar smoke intermingled with the fragrance of hot roast beef and hops. When manure from a nervous young horse hits the ground, a valet in an immaculate white coat with a broom and waste tin materializes to whisk it away, though often not before its scent adds its weight to the already heavy air. At the crowded bars, horse people keep the bartenders busy splashing relief from the heat and tension over fast-melting squares of ice. The cadence of accents from the Middle East, Asia, England, Ireland, France, and other distant lands mixes with the hiss of whispers into an alluring, foreign melody. The whole place reeks of the money and raw power crammed between its walls.

When I was working the sales, there were only a few female horse handlers, and we were appraised with the same calculated lust directed at the fillies and colts. The attention swept me back into my first paying job as I felt those large stallion eyes on me once more. One by one the handlers walked their yearlings up and back the bluestone path, then stood their animals square while buyers examined them from all sides and ran a hand up a leg or two to check the auction lot's soundness for racing. Sharing the spotlight amid the smells and sounds and sensations gave rise to my own animal instincts. No longer did I giggle as I had in the stallion's stall over the sensuous pleasures that others took and that I was beginning to desire for myself. How could I? I loved horses. From my earliest days in the barn at Hartland, they had brought my senses to life.

From: MUSIC AND SILENCE

Rose Tremain

He agrees to the ride.

He agrees because he likes the idea of galloping fast through the Frederiksborg woods, to their limits and beyond, as if running away from his life. If he cannot escape to the New World, such as he dreamed of on the night he heard the story of the execution, at least he can ride until he's exhausted and find some kind of oblivion in that.

He chooses strong horses, giving no thought to how Francesca will manage her spirited mount, because in his imagination he has already left her far behind and is alone in his own part of the forest. And he rides on until he knows that he's lost. And in this feeling of being lost is a kind of rapture.

Francesca wears a riding cloak and hat of black velvet.

Under the lightless sky, her face appears pale, her eyes large, her lips dark. She instructs the groom to spread out her cloak behind her and Peter Claire notes the care with which the man accomplishes this task, as though his hands had never touched velvet before, never saddled a horse for any woman as beautiful as Countess O'Fingal.

This beauty of hers—which she perfects first in the rearrangement of the cloak and then in the way she sits tall and straight and unafraid on her horse—Peter Claire sees as a studied reproach to him. It asks him how he can be so miserly as to resist her. It reminds him that enchantment very often triumphs over scruple and will continue to do so for as long as the world lasts.

They ride fast, just as Peter Claire had imagined they would, except that Francesca keeps up with him stride for stride, and when he glances at her he sees that she is almost laughing, and this remembered sound of her laughter is as potent as music.

So it is he who reins in his horse first and slows to a canter and then a trot. They are approaching a clearing, to which Francesca gallops on. She doesn't stop, nor even slow down, only calls to him to catch her up again. Clearly, the speed of the ride thrills her and she wants to go on at this daring pace.

And thus the gallop now becomes a kind of chase, in which Peter Claire has to use his whip, and it seems to him that Francesca, with her cloak billowing out in the air, is determined to outdistance him. For a moment, as the path turns northwards, he considers letting go and idling here until she chooses to return, but pride forces him to keep following, pride and a kind of rising elation and a sudden insatiable curiosity, as though the Countess were leading him to some destination that only she is capable of finding.

His horse begins to sweat, but Peter Claire knows it will not falter when it starts to tire. These are the same Arabians the King uses for the tilting competitions, descendants of those he once rode in these woods with Bror Brorson. They are as edgy and strong as dancers, with sinewy hearts and delicate feet. They will let themselves be ridden until they fall.

And the woods themselves, so beloved by Christian for the wild boar hunts, spread out for miles around Frederiksborg. The paths go on and on. A man could ride in them all day and not reach their limit. So Peter Claire understands that there will be no reprieve—not yet—on this winter morning. There are only those things which define the moment, those things which play with time, giving it a frenzied, dreamlike acceleration: the spur, the whip, the pumping blood, the pursuit.

Then, at last, ahead of him as he turns a wide corner, he sees that the Countess has pulled up her horse and dismounted, and is unfastening her cloak and laying it on the ground. She stands, triumphant, waiting for him.

He leans on his horse's neck, trying to catch his breath. And, as Francesca seems to have predicted, he can't take his eyes from her. She removes some fastening from her hair and it falls free, just as she wore it at Cloyne, when they ran along the beach, following Giulietta's hoop.

Laughing, she says: "Did I tell you I had a suitor? His name is Sir Lawrence de Vere. Did I tell you that he is very rich and that I was thinking of marrying him?"

Perhaps it is the laughter or perhaps it is the mention of another man, but it is at this moment that Peter Claire knows that he has lost the battle to resist Francesca. He will go to his mistress now and she will be his mistress again and his desire for her will put everything and everyone else from his mind.

A REDUNDANCY OF HORSES

Russell Edson

There was a horse that had learned to ride other horses.

It's redundant, said the stable master's wife.

The stable master turned to his horse and said, it's redundant.

She said, and a horse riding a horse seems...

Sensually endowed, said the stable master to his horse.

Will you stop repeating everything I say before I say it. That's an even worse redundancy than a horse riding a horse, she cried.

But...

But, nothing, she cried.

Meanwhile, the horse had saddled up a mare, and was riding her away into a deep wood...

From: BREATH

Robert Creeley

These horses are, they reflect
On us, their seeming ease
A gift to all that lives,
And looks and breathes.

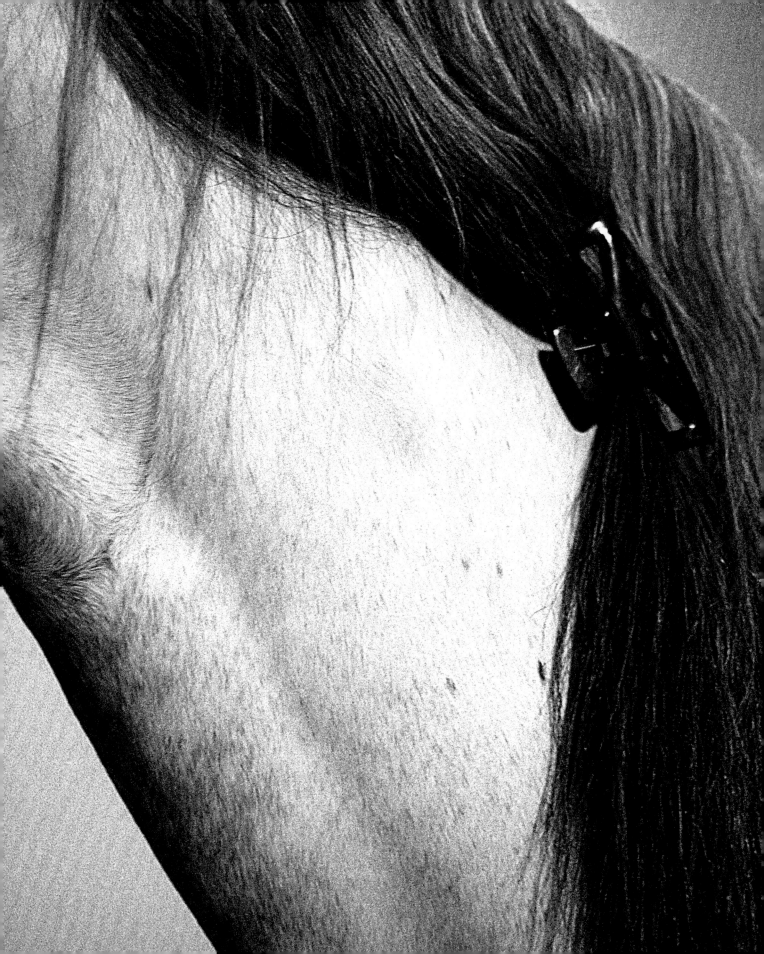

THE GRACE OF GELDINGS
IN RIPE PASTURES

Maxine Kumin

Glutted, half-asleep, browsing in
timothy grown so tall I see them
as through a pale-green stage scrim

they circle, nose to rump,
a trio of trained elephants.
It begins to rain, as promised.

Bit by bit they soak up drops
like laundry dampened to be ironed.
Runnels adorn them. Their sides

drip like the ribs of very broad
umbrellas. And still they graze
and grazing, one by one let down

their immense, indolent penises
to drench the everlasting grass
with the rich nitrogen

that repeats them.

From: INNOCENCE IN EXTREMIS

John Hawkes

*Th*e old patrician spoke. "Ladies and gentlemen," he said, "behold this horse. My dears, she is my favorite brood mare and with good reason. We are all aware of those defects that plague the horse that has been poorly bred—pawing, rushing, backing, biting, kicking, head tossing, taking the bit in her teeth, putting her head to the wind. Oh my dears, what could be worse than generations of poor breeding? But in this horse we have not a single defect. Quite the opposite. Symmetry, my dears, and balance," continued the old patrician, slowly circling the ancient groom and the oddly patient horse at which he gently and proudly gestured while he spoke, "symmetry and balance. For these she was created. For these she lives. Note well her head which is in direct proportion to the neck and is not too heavy nor too small; see the neck, which is long and muscular and flexible; look at her deep broad chest and well-sprung ribs, the loins that are short and strong, the hindquarters that are wide and symmetrical. Yes, my dears, note well the glorious muscles of these hindquarters that are so nicely rounded. Oh my dears," said the Old Gentleman, reaching up and gently stroking the broad nose, "she is a creature of intelligence, of the most refined and delicate sort of intelligence. I have only to mention that she was sired by the great Harpagon to give you an indication of her character."

Here the Old Gentleman stepped back from the waiting horse, looked upwards, clasped his hands behind his back, laughed softly and fell to musing. Then he continued.

"Here before us stands Harpagon's direct descendant. The nobility that was Harpagon's is hers. 'No feet, no horse,' is the old adage and here we have four perfect feet squarely planted beneath her body and pointing straight ahead. And look at her tail; if I gathered up the luxury of this creature's tail its silky profusion would overflow my arms! Nothing alive is more familiar to me than this brood mare, or more important. She is covered by no stallion that is not my own. I am in

personal attendance when she is covered, I am in personal attendance on each foal she drops. She is a Thoroughbred, my dears, a Thoroughbred. As are we all!

"And now," said the Old Gentleman, once more standing aside and wiping his brow, "now let her be covered!"

The privileged audience could no longer maintain its silence or contain its thrill, and began to murmur. Uncle Jake who had not understood half of what his grandfather had been saying, leaned forward and stared at the large brown horse at which his grandfather was still pointing with an imperious arm. The young equestrienne said nothing and made not a sound. As for the brood mare herself, she did not know that now her odd patience was to be rewarded and stood as she had been standing since first the privileged audience had laid eyes upon her: with her front legs somewhat forward and slightly spread; with her hind legs thrust to the rear and widely spread; and with the tail, which the Old Gentleman had praised so highly, lifted well above the straining hindquarters and swung to the side. She was patient; the heat that inflamed her from within shone in her coat; she was braced not for what she feared but for what she desired.

From far down that single corridor from the mouth of which the red curtains were tightly drawn there came the piercing sound that thrilled still more the privileged audience but shocked and frightened Uncle Jake. It was a trumpeting that could not have been made by any musical instrument, a shrieking that could not have come from the throat of a human no matter its similarity to a human cry. Again they heard it, and closer, and then, accompanied by his frantic groom, into the oval arena lunged the long-awaited stallion with tossing head, rolling eye, flying hooves, jaws wide. He kicked, he strained, he foamed, his brown coat was drenched in his desperation.

"But look there," called the Old Gentleman, who was now perspiring as freely as the stallion, "he sees her! And watch what he does, my dears. Look closely. This stallion would kill his groom in order to mount my favorite brood mare. He smells her, yet he so heeds his instinct as a great sire that he does not even know where he is or that she awaits him—despite her perfume that fills his head to bursting. He is so blind to everything except his urgency that he

cannot even recognize her for whom he yearns, her through whom he will at last discharge the genealogical dictates of no less an ancestor than the Godolphin Barb. Yes my dears, this very stallion, this carrier of the precious seed, he too is one of the distant sons of the Godolphin Barb.

"But he sees her! Now! She has appeared to him, she allays his pain. And he changes. Oh, my dears, he changes. Watch what he does. Look there!"

The Old Gentleman ceased talking. He held out both hands for quiet. And suddenly, and as if he too had heard what the Old Gentleman had said, the stallion that had been so fiercely struggling grew calm, became even timorous, and gently approached the brood mare. The blind and maddened look faded from the stallion's eye, the heaving of his chest subsided. His groom allowed the lead-rein to go slack. And in the silence the stallion came close to the brood mare where she stood for him in all her patience, and nudged her, stepped to her other side and rested his gallant head against her neck. He whinnied. He nipped her on the chest, on the neck, on the other side of the neck, then gently shoved her head with his. She stirred. He pressed his wet shoulder to her placid shoulder. He licked her neck. He turned his dark eyes upon her and whinnied.

"There!" whispered the Old Gentleman. "There we have it. The thunder of his blood is stilled—for her, for her. The stallion who cannot help the viciousness of his desire is all at once as tender as you see him now. He means both to arouse and appease the helpless creature whom in another moment he must assault. Even this great stallion, bred and born to the violence of breeding, is capable of pausing in his brute urges for the sake of his mare. The stallion is affectionate, my dears, affectionate! We honor the stallion as we do the mare!

"But wait!" cried the Old Gentleman in tones of elation as well as warning. "He mounts! He mounts! Stand back! Alert yourselves! The stallion mounts!"

Again the abrupt transformation. Again the stallion appeared to have heard and understood what the Old Gentleman had said and now behaved accordingly. Slowly, gradually, the frantic groom maneuvered his explosive charge around the brood mare, to the rear of her,

and into position. Up clamored the stallion, and slipped off. Up again and down again ungainly, undaunted, clownish and princely too in his frothing and fumbling efforts to mount the mare. The groom pushed him on one side, the Old Gentleman on the other; in silence the privileged audience urged him on. His sharp black hooves churned up the soft earth behind the mare; his every move gave vent to ruthless determination. Then up he went. And stayed. He stayed. And again the sighs of the privileged audience were audible in the arena's silence, while the Old Gentleman and the frantic groom exchanged glances and indulged in a moment's respite and the stallion, half-upended on the mare like a ship on a rock, held himself aloft in terror, his wild eyes turned upwards and fixed on the portrait of an aged stallion depicted elegantly at rest in a field. He was Harpagon, the brood mare's sire whose breeding days were done forever.

Uncle Jake squirmed in his chair. He knew without looking that there was still not a flicker of change in the disinterested attention with which the young equestrienne watched the shameful antics of the stallion. For all the trumpeting, and for all the Old Gentleman's speeches, had she really had eyes for anything except for the black disfigurement which, from the first, had made his grandfather's stallion not a handsome thoroughbred but a freak? Now the helpless horse was thwarted, as all could see; now his black disfigurement was like some quite separate creature to be trapped and tamed. It swelled, it swayed, it loomed as large as the very horse from which it hung. What must she think?

"My dears," said the Old Gentleman softly, wryly, and wiping his face and hands on a silk handkerchief, "even the act of grace itself may be delayed by distraction, the time of day, a hundred minor matters. They are no better than ourselves, these stately animals. But what would they do without us, my dears. How would they manage?"

So saying the Old Gentleman caressed the stallion's flank with one hand and then stooped and in the other seized the proud flesh. For an instant he held it, signet ring gleaming from the second finger of the steadying hand, and then slipped it home.

"Done!" he cried, wheeling upon his audience and wiping the instrumental hand on the handkerchief. "My dears, it is done!"

The stallion heaved.

The brood mare stood her ground.

"My dears," whispered the Old Gentleman as he watched the red curtains closing after the disappearing brood mare and her stallion, "he does not know what has happened to him. He does not know what he has done. But she does, my dears, she does. And so do we."

THE BUCKING HORSE MOON

Paul Zarzyski

A kiss for luck, then we'd let 'er buck—
I'd spur electric on adrenaline and lust.
    She'd figure-8 those barrels
on her Crimson Missile sorrel—
    we'd make the night air swirl with hair and dust.

At some sagebrushed wayside, 3 A.M.,
we'd water, grain, and ground-tie Missile.
    Zip our sleeping bags together,
make love in any weather,
    amid the cactus, rattlers, and thistle.

Seems the moon was always full for us—
it's high-diving shadow kicking hard.
    We'd play kid games on the big night sky,
she'd say "that bronco's Blue-Tail Fly,
    and ain't that ol' J.T. spurrin' off its stars?"

We knew sweet youth's no easy keeper.
It's spent like winnings, all too soon.
    So we'd revel every minute
in the music of our Buick
    running smooth, two rodeoin' lovers
cruising to another—
    beneath Montana's blue roan
bucking horse moon.

The Augusta show at 2, we'd place again,
then sneak off to our secret Dearborn River spot.
    We'd take some chips and beer and cheese,
skinny-dip, dry off in the breeze,
    build a fire, fry the trout we caught.

Down moonlit gravel back to blacktop,
she'd laugh and kill those beams for fun.
    That old wagon road was ours to own—
30 shows since I'd been thrown
    and 87 barrels since she'd tipped one.

    We knew that youth won't keep for rainy days.
It burns and turns to ash too soon.
    So we'd revel every minute
in the music of our Buick
    running smooth, two rodeoin' lovers
cruising to another—
    beneath Montana's blue roan
bucking horse moon.

From: HORSE HEAVEN

Jane Smiley

Now the jockeys came out of their room like a flock of tropical birds, and the horses moved out in order to the walking ring. Al and Dick were walking along together behind the horse, and Rosalind felt herself momentarily look at them as if she were a stranger, one of the bettors. They looked confident and enviable—relaxed and chatting while a sparkling, beautiful large creature radiated life right in front of them. They looked as though you could ask of them, how could they have so much of all the good things in the world that they could ignore this one? Their very relaxation in the presence of what excited everyone else set them apart and made them attractive. The jockeys were like the horses and the men both. They chatted, like the men, didn't look at the horses, like the men, but their bodies were alive and full of contained grace and spring, like the horses' bodies. They acted deferential to the trainers and the owners, but it was just the noblesse oblige that life accorded to money, that was all. The horses paused in their circle, and the trainers threw the jockeys into their saddles.

Back up in the box, Dick sat with them as the horses came out onto the track and began their slow trek around to the starting gate. The race was a mile. The starting gate was down the track to their left, being set in place. Rosalind looked at it for a moment, then turned her head and looked at Dick Winterson, who had been training their horses for some three years now. She was perfectly familiar with Dick. She saw him every month or so. They had spoken cordially time and time again, and she had hardly noticed him. Now he gazed intently at the line of horses moving out with the ponies, and he transformed before her very eyes. He wasn't paying a bit of attention to her, was thinking some sort of enigmatic horse-trainer's thoughts, God knew what those could be, but they would be something expert and focused and habitual—that thought gave her a little shiver. His eyes were brown, she noticed, and he didn't wear glasses, and he had a nice rather beaky nose. Something she had truly never noticed before was that he had lovely lips, neatly cut but full and soft-looking. At this Rosalind looked away, but then she looked back. When she looked back, and this was the turning point, she knew that he was, underneath everything, sad about something, and she felt her little appetite of the morning suddenly burst through her body so that she had to sit back and pick Eileen up again and pet her. And she sneezed. She sneezed three times. Dick Winterson said, "Do you have a cold?"

"No, not that I know of."

In Rosalind's view, those were the first words they ever spoke to one another. This was the moment when, afterwards, it seemed to Rosalind that she had cast her spell. There seemed nothing voluntary about it. It was more as if her wish that she hardly knew yet was a wish went out of her and re-created the world. The first thing that happened was that the horses arrived at the starting gate and loaded in, one by one, with Laurita routinely doing her job, as all Dick's horses did, because they were well trained and well prepared. Then there was that pause, so short, of equine uniformity, as all eight animals stood in a row. Then the bell clanged and the gate opened. Right then, Rosalind felt, she created the race of a lifetime. Six of the horses got away well, and Laurita might have also, but the number-three horse stumbled as the gate opened, and half fell into her path. The filly did an amazing thing—she launched herself and her jockey over the head and neck of the stumbling horse in a graceful bascule, and took off after the others. Everyone in the stands gasped, for the action was taking place right in front of them. Dick gasped himself, then chuckled in relief, and said to Al, "Those Northern Babys can jump, all right! Little did you know when you sent that mare to him! Ha!" But then he fell silent, they all fell silent, as the filly ran down the field as if they were standing still. She overtook them one by one, her stride seeming to lengthen by the second. And she hadn't ever been a heroic filly. It was as if the jump over the other horse told her who she was, and now she was glorying in it. Halfway down the backstretch, she was in the lead by a neck. The other filly, a rangy gray, was the favorite, and had already won over half a million dollars to Laurita's $104,000. And the other filly was a fighter. She matched Laurita stride for stride. Even though she had created this race, Rosalind didn't herself understand it. It looked to her as though the gray, bigger, longer-legged, more experienced, more mature, more expensive, and better bred, would surely press her natural claims and take the race. They were head and head around the second turn and into the homestretch. Laurita was on the outside, and the other filly had the rail. They looked pasted together. The rest of the field was nowhere, and the grandstand was roaring, every bettor, no matter whom he or she had bet upon, screaming in joy. Now the jockeys went to their whips. But it was no contest. Laurita found another gear so easily it seemed she hadn't even looked for it. She simply drew away from the bigger filly, opened up daylight, and crossed the finish line by herself. The jockey had stopped with his whip, had lost his whip. Now he stood up in his stirrups, transfigured, his mouth open, his whip hand in the air. Later when they published the photo of him

in the *Thoroughbred Times*, you almost couldn't look at it, since the wonderment of eleven thousand onlookers was concentrated in his visage. Dick said, "I never saw anything like that in my whole life."

Then they all got up and came together in the winner's circle, horse and jockey, trainer, groom, owner, owner's wife. A few weeks later, they got the win picture. Rosalind taped it up in her bathroom. She looked at it often, pondering the blank look on everyone's face. Every human face, that is. The filly looked bright and interested, as if she had just awakened from a long, sleepy dream.

Their group left the stands right after that. Even the jockey, who had a mount in the eighth race, left, not because he didn't want to ride the horse, but because he forgot what he was doing for about four hours.

They followed the filly under the stands, through the walking ring, back to the test barn. The whole way was paved by a sea of smiling faces and shouts of "Great job! Wow! What a filly!" Al said nothing, rendered speechless for the first time in Rosalind's experience. Dick said nothing, either. And, of course, Rosalind said nothing. She was a quiet sort of person. But her powers were in full flood. Every time she looked at Dick, he looked at her and she didn't turn her eyes away and neither did he. She fancied that he knew she had made this race for him, to relieve his sadness, and now his sadness was relieved. Al never saw them look at each other, either. That was another thing she did. The last thing in the world she wanted to do was hurt Al.

When the filly had been put in her stall, taken care of in every way possible, and then left alone to contemplate her greatness, Al said to Dick, "Dinner? Champagne? I'll treat everyone. You round 'em up and I'll get the limo. Rosalind, you pick the restaurant, and call for a private room." Al was really happy—that registered. In the limo, back at the hotel, he caroled about plans, the way he always did when he was happy. "Rossy! That filly's got Breeders' Cup written all over her. You know how I feel about the Breeders' Cup. I am a breeder! All the breeders, that's their test, the Breeders' Cup. Seven races, what is that, seventy horses, the best Thoroughbreds, of all kinds, colts, fillies, sprinters, turf horses. There's nothing like it. I always said there's nothing like it anywhere in the world, didn't I? You know I did! This filly—" But she smiled and nodded and listened and said, "Maybe so,

Al, maybe." Maybe. That was an interesting word. Maybeness was something rather unusual for her.

It wasn't hard getting a private room for twenty at the best restaurant in Boca Raton, then transporting the whole crew—grooms, hot walkers, assistants, the woman who did the books, Eileen, everyone—over there, no matter what languages they spoke or what they were wearing. Smiles and welcome followed them everywhere. They drank Perrier-Jouët and ate pesto risotto with scallops, then ate osso bucco and veal piccata, and then the limos took everyone away drunk, and Al's cellular rang, and it was his partner, saying that Al had to get the late plane back to the City, because there was some fuckup in Croatia, where they had a factory, and so Al himself left, and there they were, Rosalind and Dick, sitting alone, except for Eileen, across from each other at a table littered with the remains of a very very good party. Eileen sat in the chair next to Rosalind, directly across from Dick. Her ears were forward and she was looking at him expectantly, and it seemed to Rosalind that he and she, the humans, could at last do what both of them had been longing to do for hours, which was to stare straight into each other's faces without stopping or turning away or speaking or wondering who might see them. Already, Dick's face was as familiar to Rosalind as her own. And his familiar face had a strange look on it, a scowl-like look that was not a scowl but a look of intense feeling—his inner life emerging unprotected into the rosy candlelight of the room. She was far more careful of her own look. She tried to make it almost blank, almost a mask, so that he would have to come out farther, reveal himself more, just to get a rise out of her. You would think she did this all the time, but she didn't. In her eighteen years with Al, she had considered it beneath her dignity even to flirt with another man. And she didn't intend to flirt with Dick, either. If he came toward her, it would have to be on his own, without encouragement. The appetite that had detonated inside her that afternoon was not for fun or amusement. It was for something mysterious and testing. No man, she thought, should be lured to that through the false advertising of a smile or a toss of the head. She thought of Nefertiti, making herself look like that, and she waited. Eileen was thinking of something, too. She put her forefeet on the table and drank delicately from a goblet of mineral water.

"Ah," Dick said. "Rosalind. Thank you for the party. Everyone really had a terrific time."

"Did they? Good." Eileen sat back down.

"I mean it. This is not a world that most of them—"

"It was Al's idea. Al is a generous man, in his way. Sometimes that isn't an obvious way, I admit." Now she permitted herself a smile.

The next thing he said would show, she thought, that he had made a choice, and she didn't dare influence that choice in one way or another. She guessed he would say something like "Well, then," or "Late, for me," or "Where can I drop you?" Perhaps all of those remarks passed through his mind, unselected. At any rate, he said, "You have beautiful hair."

She nodded.

"And beautiful eyes."

She nodded.

"And beautiful lips."

"All original equipment," she said, "even the hair. No one in my family goes gray."

"Yours is…" He shook his head. "I don't know, sunny. Sandy. Palomino! Ha!" He smiled in a friendly way, but he had let the cry out, no mistake about it. Rosalind took a deep breath, and then Dick said, "Where are you staying?" Eileen began to pant.

"I think Al was at the Meridian. We've bought a condo recently, but I haven't finished furnishing it yet."

Then he said, "Let's go there."

Then she said, "Let's."

What she could tell when he was taking down her hair, and then unbuttoning her jacket and her blouse, was how many years he had spent with horses. His gestures were smooth and consistent, and once he had his hands on her body, he kept them there. But they weren't eager and hungry; they were quiet and reassuring, warm, dry, and knowledgeable, as if he could find out things about her by touching her, the way he would have to do with horses, the way, perhaps, he would do with Laurita tomorrow, running his hands down her legs looking for heat. His touch, in fact, belied the look on his face, which was disturbed and eager. His touch was almost idle. When he had his hand on her neck, she felt him probe a little knot there, press it and release it, the way her masseuse did, then move down to her shoulder, and do the same there. It was as if no degree of desire could interfere with his habit of taking care. They had been naked for ten minutes when she spoke for the first time. She said, "I bet the horses like you." Eileen, who had been lying curled on the bed, jumped down and went under the bedskirt.

"They seem to, actually."

"You have a nice touch."

"I get along well with dogs, too. Though Eileen hasn't really made up to me."

"And you don't get along with…?"

"Owners, maybe."

"Al likes you."

He looked her right in the eye. "Oh, they like me all right. I don't like them."

Rosalind threw back her head and laughed.

"And I don't get along with my wife."

"Is that why you look sad?"

"No doubt. Do I look sad, then?"

"You do to me."

He sighed. "I've been afraid it would get out."

"You looked happy after the race. Well, not happy, but excited. Almost happy."

"I was almost happy. Closest I've been in a pretty long time. She's a bombshell, that filly." Here was where Rosalind fell in love, because Dick had a whole different smile for this filly when he thought of her, a whole separate category of secret delight that crossed his face and pierced Rosalind for some reason she didn't begin to understand. She had been looking for mystery, hadn't she? Well, here it was.

Even so, they could still stop, get dressed, turn back. Their friendly conversation and her laugh showed that. In the atmosphere of the room, there was some levity, some detachment, some pure friendliness that they could build upon to get out of this. Rosalind knew it. But instead she put her fingertips on his lips and ran them gently around, a multitude of her nerve endings tickling a multitude of his. And then she leaned forward, letting her hair fall on his shoulders, and kissed him.

Maybe he wasn't getting along with his wife, but it was obvious that he had gotten along with her fine at some point, or with someone else, because his knowledge about what to do with Rosalind was instinctive and expert. First, he took her face between his hands and very gently and attentively ran his thumbs over her eyebrows, the planes of her cheeks, down the line of her jaw, bringing them to a rest upon her lips, where, after just a moment, he put the tips of them into her mouth. She could feel him touching her tongue and the inside of her lips. Then he smoothed that moisture into her cheeks and chin, over and over, until she was groaning. Then he ran one hand lightly down her throat, reminding her what a long and vulnerable throat it was. Then the other hand. Then he looked at her and kissed her, first just soft kissing, then firmer kissing, then tongue kissing, then gently biting her lips, kissing, biting, kissing, then kissing her neck, then biting, then kissing. Except the bites weren't bites, so careful and considerate were they, as if he were inside her skin and knew exactly what would be exciting and what would be painful. He bit her shoulders, left, then right. Meanwhile, his hands had found her breasts. Al's hands always happened upon her breasts as if he had never felt breasts before, but Dick's hands knew breasts perfectly well, and hers, it seemed, in particular. Pretty soon, but not too soon, his lips found them, too. She closed her eyes, because she didn't want to look at anything but his face now. His face was the only familiar thing in the room, and if she couldn't look at it, then what was happening in her body was too terrifying. Her body was already arching and shaking, but she wasn't orgasming. She was just responding to the lightness of his touch like iron filings to a magnet.

Now his hands moved downward, to her waist. She had not known the waist was an especially erogenous zone, but as he squeezed her waist and ran his thumbs and hands over her belly, she felt her whole lower body turn to fire, and sparks shoot out of her toes. It was as if there were some spot there, near her navel, that was sensitive and he knew it, he knew just where it was and how to activate it. She

opened her eyes now, and saw that his eyes were closed, and that furthermore, she was participating unbeknownst to herself. She was rhythmically pinching his nipples, and he liked it. His hands fell away from her waist to her buttocks, and now he wasn't so gentle with her. He squeezed them hard, over and over, pinched them too, but it didn't hurt. Always there was that quality in his touch of being unable to hurt living flesh. It was alluring, but more than that, it was fascinating. While this was going on, she opened her eyes again, and he was looking at her. He looked happy and fond. The look made her moan, because she didn't feel that she deserved fondness from him. Suddenly, and very very lightly, he touched her labia so that she cried out, and as she was crying out, he penetrated her, kindly but firmly, threw back his head, closed his own eyes, seeming to pull her over himself as easily as a glove.

He penetrated her to the core, didn't he? He knew just how to do that, the way a racehorse knew how to find the finish line: wherever he penetrated her to, that was the core, and she felt it. He eased gently back and forth a time or two, and it wasn't so comfortable just then, but right when she was going to say something, or ask something, she got a wonderful feeling of moisture flooding her, and his penis turning to silk inside of her. She said, "What was that?"

And he said, "Sometimes it takes a moment or two for the foreskin to slide back."

"You have a foreskin?"

"I do, indeed. I was born in Britain when my father was training horses there for some years."

"I'm sorry I didn't notice. I guess I was looking at your face."

He smiled.

But then there was no time for talking, only for probing more and more deeply into this feeling she was having all through her body of melting around him as he went farther inside of her, and just when she orgasmed, he covered her face with his warm hands and made her go where he was inside her and she disappeared.

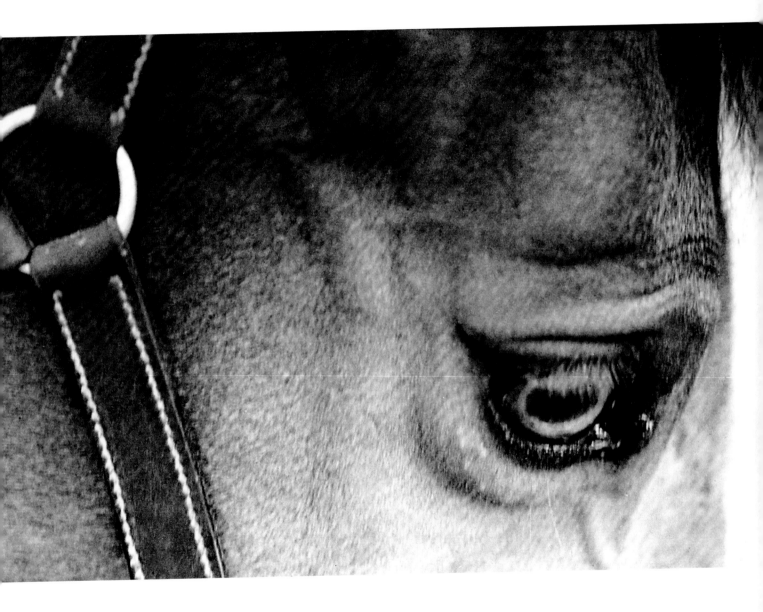

YONDER

Heartbreak & Haven

I've spent most of my life riding horses.
The rest I've just wasted.

—Anonymous

ICE HORSES

Joy Harjo

These are the ones who escape
after the last hurt is turned inward;
they are the most dangerous ones.
These are the hottest ones,
but so cold that your tongue sticks
to them and is torn apart because it is
frozen to the motion of hooves.
These are the ones who cut your thighs,
whose blood you must have seen on the gloves
of the doctor's rubber hands. They are
the horses who moaned like oceans, and
one of them a young woman screamed aloud;
she was the only one.
These are the ones who have found you.
These are the ones who pranced on your belly.
They chased deer out of your womb.
These are the ice horses, horses
who entered through your head,
and then your heart,
your beaten heart.

These are the ones who loved you.
They are the horses who have held you
so close that you have become
a part of them,
         an ice horse
galloping
      into fire.

TWENTY MINUTES

James Salter

*Th*is happened near Carbondale to a woman named Jane Vare. I
met her once at a party. She was sitting on a couch with her
arms stretched out on either side and a drink in one hand. We talked
about dogs.

She had an old greyhound. She'd bought him to save his life, she
said. At the tracks they put them down rather than feed them when
they stopped winning, sometimes three or four together, threw them
in the back of a truck and drove to the dump. This dog was named
Phil. He was stiff and nearly blind, but she admired his dignity. He
sometimes lifted his leg against the wall, almost as high as the door
handle, but he had a fine face.

Tack on the kitchen table, mud on the wide-board floor. In she
strode like a young groom in a worn jacket and boots. She had what
they called a good seat and ribbons layered like feathers on the wall.
Her father had lived in Ireland where they rode into the dining room
on Sunday morning and the host died fallen on the bed in full attire.
Her own life had become like that. Money and dents in the side of her
nearly new Swedish car. Her husband had been gone for a year.

Around Carbondale the river drops down and widens. There's a spi-
dery trestle bridge, many times repainted, and they used to mine coal.

It was late in the afternoon and a shower had passed. The light was
silvery and strange. Cars emerging from the rain drove with their headlights on and the windshield wipers going. The yellow road machinery
parked along the shoulder seemed unnaturally bright.

It was the hour after work when irrigation water glistens high in the
air, the hills have begun to darken, and the meadows are like ponds.

She was riding alone up along the ridge. She was on a horse named
Fiume, big, well formed, but not very smart. He didn't hear things and
sometimes stumbled when he walked. They had gone as far as the
reservoir and then come back, riding to the west where the sun was

going down. He could run, this horse. His hooves were pounding. The back of her shirt was filled with wind, the saddle was creaking, his huge neck was dark with sweat. They came along the ditch and toward a gate—they jumped it all the time.

At the last moment something happened. It took just an instant. He may have crossed his legs or hit a hole but he suddenly gave way. She went over his head and as if in slow motion he came after. He was upside down—she lay there watching him float toward her. He landed on her open lap.

It was as if she'd been hit by a car. She was stunned but felt unhurt. For a minute she imagined she might stand up and brush herself off.

The horse had gotten up. His legs were dirty and there was dirt on his back. In the silence she could hear the clink of the bridle and even the water flowing in the ditch. All around her were meadows and stillness. She felt sick to her stomach. It was all broken down there—she knew it although she could feel nothing. She knew she had some time. Twenty minutes, they always said.

The horse was pulling at some grass. She rose to her elbows and was immediately dizzy. "God damn you!" she called. She was nearly crying. "Git! Go home!" Someone might see the empty saddle. She closed her eyes and tried to think. Somehow she could not believe it—nothing that had happened was true.

It was that way the morning they came and told her Privet had been hurt. The foreman was waiting in the pasture. "Her leg's broken," he said.

"How did it happen?"

He didn't know. "It looks like she got kicked," he guessed.

The horse was lying under a tree. She knelt and stroked its board-like nose. The large eyes seemed to be looking elsewhere. The vet would be driving up from Catherine Store trailing a plume of dust, but it turned out to be a long time before he came. He parked a little way off and walked over. Afterward he said what she had known he would say, they were going to have to put her down.

She lay remembering that. The day had ended. Lights were appearing in parts of distant houses. The six o'clock news was on. Far below she could see the hayfield of Piñones and much closer, a hundred yards off, a truck. It belonged to someone trying to build a house down there. It was up on blocks, it didn't run. There were other houses within a mile or so. On the other side of the ridge the metal roof, hidden in trees, of old man Vaughn who had once owned all of this and now could hardly walk. Further west the beautiful tan adobe Bill Millinger built before he went broke or whatever it was. He had wonderful taste. The house had the peeled log ceilings of the Southwest, Navajo rugs, and fireplaces in every room. Wide views of the mountains through windows of tinted glass. Anyone who knew enough to build a house like that knew everything.

She had given the famous dinner for him, unforgettable night. The clouds had been blowing off the top of Sopris all day, then came the snow. They talked in front of the fire. There were wine bottles crowded on the mantel and everyone in good clothes. Outside the snow poured down. She was wearing silk pants and her hair was loose. In the end she stood with him near the doorway to her kitchen. She was filled with warmth and a little drunk, was he?

He was watching her finger on the edge of his jacket lapel. Her heart thudded. "You're not going to make me spend the night alone?" she asked.

He had blond hair and small ears close to his head. "Oh…" he began.

"What?"

"Don't you know? I'm the other way."

Which way, she insisted. It was such a waste. The roads were almost closed, the house lost in snow. She began to plead—she couldn't help it—and then became angry. The silk pants, the furniture, she hated it all.

In the morning his car was outside. She found him in the kitchen making breakfast. He'd slept on the couch, combed his longish hair with his fingers. On his cheeks was a blond stubble. "Sleep well, darling?" he asked.

Sometimes it was the other way around—in Saratoga in the bar where the idol was the tall Englishman who had made so much money at the sales. Did she live there? he asked. When you were close his eyes looked watery but in that English voice which was so pure, "It's marvelous to come to a place and see someone like you," he said.

She hadn't really decided whether to stay or leave and she had a drink with him. He smoked a cigarette.

"You haven't heard about those?" she said.

"No, what about them?"

"They'll give thee cancer."

"Thee?"

"It's what the Quakers say."

"Are you really a Quaker?"

"Oh, back a ways."

He had her by the elbow. "Do you know what I'd like? I'd like to fuck thee," he said.

She bent her arm to remove it.

"I mean it," he said. "Tonight."

"Some other time," she told him.

"I don't have another time. My wife's coming tomorrow, I only have tonight."

"That's too bad. I have every night."

She hadn't forgotten him, though she'd forgotten his name. His shirt had elegant blue stripes. "Oh, damn you," she suddenly cried. It was the horse. He hadn't gone. He was over by the fence. She began to call him, "Here, boy. Come here," she begged. He wouldn't move.

She didn't know what to do. Five minutes had passed, perhaps longer. Oh, God, she said, oh, Lord, oh God our Father. She could see the long stretch of road that came up from the highway, the unpaved surface very pale. Someone would come up that road and not turn off. The disastrous road. She had been driving it that day with her husband. There was something he had been meaning to tell her, Henry said, his head tilted back at a funny angle. He was making a change in his life. Her heart took a skip. He was breaking off with Mara, he said.

There was silence.

Finally she said, "With who?"

He realized his mistake. "The girl who… in the architect's office. She's the draftsman."

"What do you mean, breaking it off?" It was hard for her to speak. She was looking at him as one would look at a fugitive.

"You knew about that, didn't you? I was sure you knew. Anyway it's over. I wanted to tell you. I wanted to put it all behind us."

"Stop the car," she said. "Don't say any more, stop here."

He drove alongside her trying to explain but she was picking up the biggest stones she could find and throwing them at the car. Then she cut unsteadily across the fields, the sage bushes scratching her legs.

When she heard him drive up after midnight she jumped from bed and shouted from the window, "No, no! Go away!"

"What I never understood is why no one told me," she used to say. "They were supposed to be my friends."

Some failed, some divorced, some got shot in trailers like Doug Portis who had the excavation business and was seeing the policeman's wife. Some like her husband moved to Santa Barbara and became the extra man at dinner parties.

It was growing dark. Help me, someone, help me, she kept repeating. Someone would come, they had to. She tried not to be afraid. She thought of her father who could explain life in one sentence. "They knock you down and you get up. That's what it's all about." He recognized only one virtue. He would hear what had happened, that she merely lay there. She had to try to get home, even if she went only a little way, even a few yards.

Pushing with her palms she managed to drag herself, calling the horse as she did. Perhaps she could grab a stirrup if he came. She tried to find him. In the last of the light she saw the fading cottonwoods but the rest had disappeared. The fence posts were gone. The meadows had drifted away.

She tried to play a game, she wasn't lying near the ditch, she was in another place, in all the places, on Eleventh Street in that first apartment above the big skylight of the restaurant, the morning in Sausalito with the maid knocking on the door and Henry trying to call in Spanish, not now, not now! And postcards on the marble of the dresser and things they'd bought. Outside the hotel in Haiti the cabdrivers were leaning on their cars and calling out in soft voices, Hey, *blanc*, you like to go to a nice beach? Ibo beach? They wanted thirty dollars for the day, they said, which meant the price was probably about five. Go ahead, give it to him, she said. She could be there so easily, or in

her own bed reading on a stormy day with the rain gusting against the window and the dogs near her feet. On the desk were photographs: horses, and her jumping, and one of her father at lunch outside when he was thirty, at Burning Tree. She had called him one day—she was getting married, she said. Married, he said, to whom? A man named Henry Vare, she said, who is wearing a beautiful suit, she wanted to add, and has wonderful wide hands. Tomorrow, she said.

"Tomorrow?" He sounded farther away. "Are you sure you're doing the right thing?"

"Absolutely."

"God bless you," he said.

That summer was the one they came here—it was where Henry had been living—and bought the place past the Macraes'. All year they fixed up the house and Henry started his landscaping business. They had their own world. Up through the fields in nothing but shorts, the earth warm under their feet, skin flecked with dirt from swimming in the ditch where the water was chilly and deep, like two sun-bleached children but far better, the screen door slamming, things on the kitchen table, catalogues, knives, new everything. Autumn with its brilliant blue skies and the first storms coming up from the west.

It was dark now, everywhere except up by the ridge. There were all the things she had meant to do, to go East again, to visit certain friends, to live a year by the sea. She could not believe it was over, that she was going to be left here on the ground.

Suddenly she started to call for help, wildly, the cords standing out in her neck. In the darkness the horse raised his head. She kept shouting. She already knew it was a thing she would pay for, she was loosing the demonic. At last she stopped. She could hear the pounding of her heart and beyond that something else. Oh, God, she began to beg. Lying there she heard the first solemn drumbeats, terrible and slow.

Whatever it was, however bad, I'm going to do it as my father would, she thought. Hurriedly she tried to imagine him and as she was doing it a length of something went through her, something iron. In one unbelievable instant she realized the power of it, where it would take her, what it meant.

Her face was wet and she was shivering. Now it was here. Now you must do it, she realized. She knew there was a God, she hoped it. She shut her eyes. When she opened them it had begun, so utterly unforeseen and with such speed. She saw something dark moving along the fence line. It was her pony, the one her father had given her long ago, her black pony going home, across the broad fields, across the grassland. Wait, wait for me!

She began to scream.

Lights were jerking up and down along the ditch. It was a pickup coming over the uneven ground, the man who was sometimes building the lone house and a high school girl named Fern who worked at the golf course. They had the windows up and, turning, their lights swept close to the horse but they didn't see him. They saw him later, coming back in silence, the big handsome face in the darkness looking at them dumbly.

"He's saddled," Fern said in surprise.

He was standing calmly. That was how they found her. They put her in the back—she was limp, there was dirt in her ears—and drove into Glenwood at eighty miles an hour, not even stopping to call ahead.

That wasn't the right thing, as someone said later. It would have been better if they had gone the other way, about three miles up the road to Bob Lamb's. He was the vet but he might have done something. Whatever you said, he was the best doctor around.

They would have pulled in with the headlights blooming on the white farmhouse as happened so many nights. Everyone knew Bob Lamb. There were a hundred dogs, his own among them, buried in back of the barn.

FOR A SHETLAND PONY BROOD MARE WHO DIED IN HER BARREN YEAR

Maxine Kumin

After bringing forth eighteen
foals in as many Mays
you might, old Trinket girl,
have let yourself be lulled
this spring into the green days
of pasture and first curl
of timothy. Instead,
your milk bag swelled again,
an obstinate machine.
Your long pale tongue
waggled in every feed box.
You slicked your ears back
to scatter other mares
from the salt lick.
You were full of winter burdocks
and false pregnancy.

By midsummer all the foals
had breached, except the ghost
you carried. In the bog
where you came down each noon
to ease your deer-thin hoofs in mud,
a jack-in-the-pulpit cocked
his overhang like a question mark.
We saw come autumn soon
that botflies would take your skin
and bloodworms settle
inside the cords and bands
that laced your belly,
your church of folded hands.

But all in good time, Trinket!
Was it something you understood?
Full of false pride
you lay down and died
in the sun,
all silken on one side,
all mud on the other one.

From: THE FINISH

Sir Alfred Munnings

I was like a thirsty man let loose in a cellar: I became drunk with riding. I hung up a large ordnance map, covering half a wall, and explored a different part of the country each day, going a week later to see if I had forgotten the route…

What rides! and what respite, resting by a running stream at the bottom of a far-off combe, eating food out of a paper bag, and afterwards drinking from the stream. Now and again I would invite a colonel of those Hussars who wear red breeches—Henry I shall call him, a fine horseman, a lightweight and good companion—to ride one of the horses and come out for the day; a whole day on the moors. Both of us, well on in years, started out forty-five years younger. For a day we were boys, on better horses than we would have ridden at fifteen. But we were not older than fifteen in our ways, and we had no better sense, except in judging the boggy tracts. Imagine a scene on the lonely, desolate, rock-strewn moor beyond Simonsbath… A dip in the ground; gorse and patches of heather; rough stone walls and, lower in the dip, a small stone farmhouse. We were trying to cross to Exehead, and not sure of a piece of down.

'Stop, Henry!' I cried as his horse got deeper in. 'Come round by the wall.'

'But,' said Henry, 'those cows are feeding there.'

For all that, he had to go where I went. His horse was over its knees, and not liking it. I am unable to put on paper the unrestrained feeling of utter freedom when riding out in the morning from King's; gradually getting away from farms, lanes, and enclosures. Our route let us across the Simonsbath road to a succession of wide, walled-in, downland enclosures, going on to Prayway head. The gates had long gone in that region, and fixed across the gateways were large poles keeping in the stock.

'Are you for it, Alfred?' Henry would say.

"Am I for it!' said I, and at a nice, steady canter we took the obstacles side by side with great glee.

CONFESSOR HORSE

Joan Logghe

Who can I tell my fabulous news?
Can I tell the horse, half dead,
his white coat in winter drag, ears
that flatten, his sway-back and never mind.
Can I tell him it's happening again, confessor horse,
like that night when I wore red Chinese silk,
dragons to the ground? He wore white for evening,
I made my vows before him as I waited
for the lovers to return, but they never did
so I drew my horse's profile on the mirror in Midnight Red,
added words, only a few. I was primed to cry,
my primer coat of gray hair, my long standing
understanding out with horse girls.

That's three now, each with a place
between the saddle and her legs to store
a secret. One he gave my saddle to shine.
One wanted to add spices to our shelves.
My friend said, "When I feel blue I'm never wrong."
My old horse mopes, mirror to the nag I've become.
Yesterday I rode him down the road.
Only the llamas spooked him, he who lets
pit bulls attack. But I was spooked all along.
"There's a lot of God coming out of my mouth,"
the youngest son said at his father's funeral
last week. Give me absolution, padre horse,
hear my prayer. Pray for us. We water the land
in times of drought with after thought. A lot

of God is coming. I get to ride my victim steed,
wear my drama garb, stay up all night rehearsing
for the benefit performance for this non-profit
called married life. Dear Horse, I'm glad
you don't have a cell phone to break my heart.
I rode on your strong back a dozen years,
I let you carry my heavier weight. I do not count
you among the unfaithful.

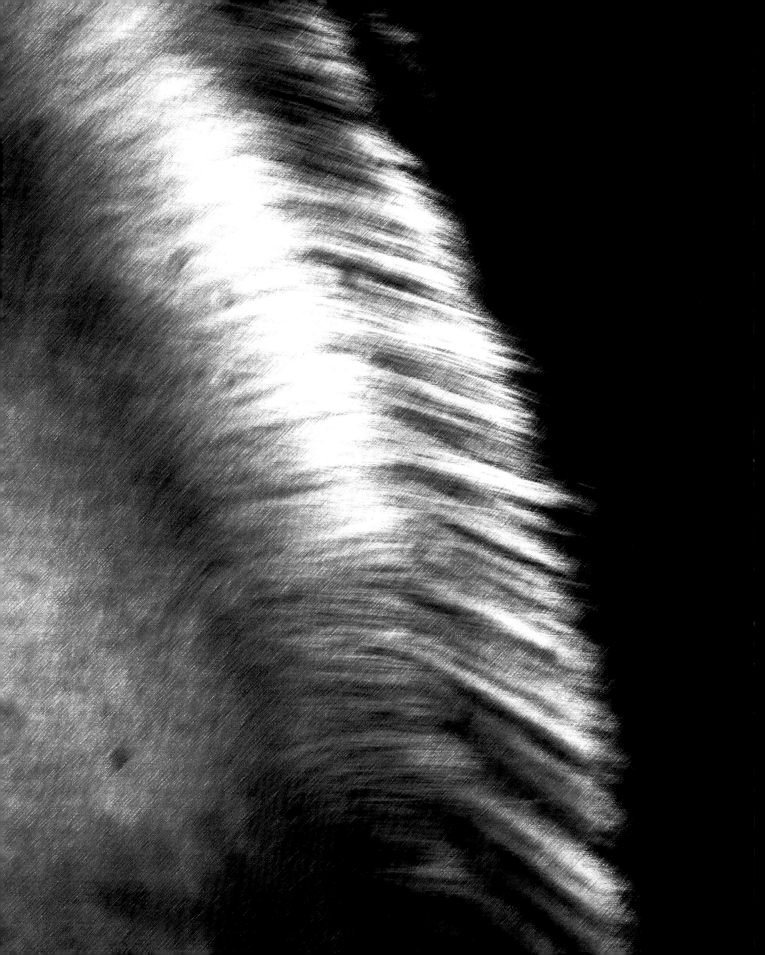

From: THE LOVER OF HORSES

Tess Gallagher

By all accounts, my great-grandfather was like a huge stallion him-self, and when he went into a field where a herd of horses was grazing, the horses would suddenly lift their heads and call to him. Then his bearded mouth would move, and though he was making sounds that could have been words, which no horse would have had reason to understand, the horses would want to hear; and one by one they would move toward him across the open space of the field. He could turn his back and walk down the road, and they would follow him. He was probably drunk my mother said, because he was swaying

and mumbling all the while. Sometimes he would stop dead-still in the road and the horses would press up against him and raise and lower their heads as he moved his lips. But because these things were only seen from a distance, and because they have eroded in the telling, it is now impossible to know whether my great-grandfather said anything of importance to the horses. Or even if it was his whispering that had brought about their good behavior. Nor was it clear, when he left them in some barnyard as suddenly as he'd come to them, whether they had arrived at some new understanding of the difficult and complex relationship between men and horses.

Only the aberrations of my great-grandfather's relationship with horses have survived—as when he would bathe in the river with his favorite horse or when, as my grandmother told my mother, he insisted on conceiving his ninth child in the stall of a bay mare named Redwing. Not until I was grown and going through the family Bible did I discover that my grandmother had been this ninth child, and so must have known something about the matter.

These oddities in behavior lead me to believe that when my great-grandfather, at the age of fifty-two, abandoned his wife and family to join a circus that was passing through the area, it was not simply drunken bravado, nor even the understandable wish to escape family obligations. I believe the gypsy in him finally got the upper hand, and it led to such a remarkable happening that no one in the family has so far been willing to admit it: not the obvious transgression—that he had run away to join the circus—but that he was in all likelihood a man who had been stolen by a horse.

This is not an easy view to sustain in the society we live in. But I have not come to it frivolously, and have some basis for my belief. For although I have heard the story of my great-grandfather's defection time and again since childhood, the one image which prevails in all versions is that of a dappled gray stallion that had been trained to dance a variation of the mazurka. So impressive was this animal that he mesmerized crowds with his sliding step-and-hop to the side through the complicated figures of the dance, which he performed, not in the way of Lippizaners—with other horses and their riders—but riderless and with the men of the circus company as his partners.

It is known that my great-grandmother became one of these dancers. After that he was reputed, in my mother's words, to have gone "completely to ruin." The fact that he walked from the house with only the clothes on his back, leaving behind his own beloved horses (twenty-nine of them to be exact), further supports my idea that a powerful force must have held sway over him, something more profound than the miseries of drink or the harsh imaginings of his abandoned wife.

Not even the fact that seven years later he returned and knocked on his wife's door, asking to be taken back, could exonerate him from what he had done, even though his wife did take him in and looked after him until he died some years later. But the detail that no one takes note of in the account is that when my great-grandfather returned, he was carrying a saddle blanket and the black plumes from the headgear of one of the circus horses. This passes by even my mother as simply a sign of the ridiculousness of my great-grandfather's plight—for after all, he was homeless and heading for old age as a "good for nothing drunk" and a "fool for horses."

No one has bothered to conjecture what these curious emblems—saddle blanket and plumes—must have meant to my great-grandfather. But he hung them over the foot of his bed—"like a fool," my mother said. And sometimes when he got very drunk he would take up the blanket and, wrapping it like a shawl over his shoulders, he would grasp the plumes. Then he would dance the mazurka. He did not dance in the living room but took himself out into the field, where the horses stood at attention and watched as if suddenly experiencing the smell of the sea or a change of wind in the valley. "Drunks don't care what they do," my mother would say as she finished her story about my great-grandfather. "Talking to a drunk is like talking to a stump."

WHEN I LOOK AT RYDER'S PAINTING, THE RACE TRACK

Lyn Lifshin

Death on a Pale
Horse, I see it reversed,
circling back. Horses
and death, the riderless
horse at JFK's
funeral, stirrups
going backward. That
May, Ruffian's
maiden, the tattoo
inside her lips
still new. I imagine
her muscles rippling
on that two
minute gallop
to the gate, the blue
air, her mane
smelling faintly of
soap and apples. Metal,
silk, the gasp, thunder,
then one black
arrow whizzing past

12 MINUTES TO POST

Charles Bukowski

as we stand there before the purple mountains
in our stupid clothing, we pause, look
about: nothing changes, it only congeals,
our lives crawl slowly, our companions depreciate us.
then
we awaken a moment—
the animals are entering the track!
Quick's Sister, Perfect Raj, Vive Le Torch,
Miss Leuschner, Keepin' Peace, True To Be,
Lou's Good Morning.

now, it's good for us: the lightning flash
of hope, the laughter of the hidden gods.
we were never meant to be what we are or where
we are, we are looking for an escape, some music
from the sun. the girl we never found.
we are betting on the miracle again
there before the purple mountains
as the horses parade past
so much more beautiful than
our lives.

A GOOD-BYE FOR MY FRIEND

PARTNERS

Drum Hadley

Old horses, women, and men,
The bones of old gone loves, now, turned out to pasture.
They were my friends, they were our partners,
They were all the long trails we rode along together,
Feet in the stirrups to gather our old beginnings,
To come to see some new way.
They were that flesh we are between our legs.
They were every cowboy's hope,
To do no work that couldn't be done a-horseback,
Feet in the stirrups, two legs dangling…
Dangling from the high withers on a horse's back,
Across the mesas and arroyos, across the mountains, the plains.
In cold times they were always the two of us together,
Tail to tail, rumps turned against the wind,
Hair frosted, soft-nosed breath to breathe into your chest,
Winds of Winter and ice, till beginning in Springtime,
We were head to tail through the dryness, the droughts,
Till in those blasts of the Summertime heat,
We were that nicker, a swish of our partner's tail,
To brush the black flies from our wet eyes away.
Now, we cross this dust to stand beside you here,
Each of us alone in this last field in the light.
We come carrying a small switch.
It is made of a leaf-stripped seep willow limb.
In this searing Summer's sun we come,
To brush the black flies,
From the corners of your wet eyes away.
Good-bye old partner.
Good-bye, those bones of old gone loves,
Still here, waiting to cross in this stillness,
Feet in the stirrups, two legs dangling…

SCRUBBING THE FLOOR THE NIGHT A GREAT LADY DIED

Ruffian 1972-1975

Jim Harrison

Sunday, with two weeks of heat lifting from us in a light rain. A good day for work with the break in the weather; then the race, the great horse faltering, my wife and daughter leaving the room in tears, the dinner strangely silent, with a dull, metallic yellow cast to the evening sun. We turn from the *repeats*, once is so much more than enough. So the event fades and late in the night writing in the kitchen I look at the floor soiled by the Airedales in the heatwave, tracking in the brackish dirt from the algae-covered pond. I want the grace of this physical gesture, filling the pail, scrubbing the floor after midnight, sweet country music from the radio and a drink or two; then the grotesque news bringing me up from the amnesia of the floor. How could a creature of such beauty merely disappear? I saw her as surely as at twilight I watched our own horses graze in the pasture. How could she wake so frantic, as if from a terrible dream? Then to continue with my scrubbing, saying it's only a horse but knowing that if I cannot care about a horse, I cannot care about earth herself. For she was so surely of earth, in earth; once so animate, sprung in some final, perfect form, running, running, saying, *"Look at me, look at me, what could be more wonderful than the way I move, tell me if there's something more wonderful, I'm the same as a great whale sounding."* But then who am I sunk on the floor scrubbing at this bitterness? It doesn't matter. A great creature died who took her body as far as bodies go toward perfection and I wonder how like Crazy Horse she seems to leave us so far behind.

From: THE CRAZY HUNTER

Kay Boyle

When they had gone from sight he walked into the dining room and although it was only just gone ten he took the decanter of whiskey out. The ordinary glasses were kept in the pantry, and sadly, quietly he thought, I cannot go out and get one any more than I can go out there and go into the stable and stop them doing it. He opened the sideboard door, stooping to it, and selected one of the small embossed porter glasses and set it on the table, and then he filled it three-quarters full with whiskey and set the decanter down, fitting the glass stopper to it, and he drank the whiskey off at once. He thought, They'll do it humanely, they're bound to do it humanely, and he looked almost peacefully at the bottom of the empty glass. If I had any arguments or any reasons to give them I could go out there, or if I could walk into the stable like a man with a wallet fat in his pocket and slap the sides of it and say, This happens to be, just happens to be my horse, not yours, my lady. He was bought by me, paid for by me, purchased under the rules of warranty (only I never got the certificate because I had two drinks instead), as sound in wind and eyes, quiet to ride, has been hunted and capable of being hunted, so pack up your chalk and your pistol and your vet, whoever he is, in your old kit bag and go back to gardening. They'll do it humanely, he thought, and the feeling of peace spread marvelously through him, something better than mere respite or truce but the final absolute conciliation through performed and indisputable act. The responsibility is being taken off my shoulders, he thought gently, forbearingly, the issue is being removed from my hands. I have no authority, no jurisdiction, even if I moved now towards the door and out it I could not save that horse, and the sense of actionless, speechless bliss rose richly in him; I am powerless, helpless because they know their business and I have none yet, I never found it; my wife will see that the target is properly indicated and the man in breeches will make use of the humane killer to the conclusion of this drama, this minor but grotesquely aggrandized tragedy which will fade slowly but unerringly into the past. It is not disaster but the one logical solution, he thought, and the voice drifted from some far dim plane of memory to hearing now, repeating as it had years back repeated all day at fifteen-minute intervals across the air, "The King's life is drawing peacefully to a close."

After the second porter-glassful was drunk, Candy put his hand to his back pocket and took his silver and leather hip-flask out. He unscrewed the cap and drew the cork out with his teeth, tipping his head on the side to do it, and then he filled it up from the decanter. He did not spill any, but because a little spread wet at the top, he ran his tongue around the screw-cap's thread, then corked the flask and twisted the top back on and slipped it under his jacket again. Or stamp down there, he thought, and take no nonsense from them, the artist out of pocket, out of luck, but painting alone, accomplishing alone experiments in style, subject, and treatment, working alone and making a name that people listen for in city exhibitions and museums, look for in catalogues and magazines, so that even a wife or even a vet's assistant would listen. He looked at the decanter in dispassionate meditation for a moment and then he filled the porter glass again. Penson drawing his last breaths, it may be, while I stand here drinking, kicked towards kingdom come and landing on the threshold, and yet I'd face my Maker saying they haven't a damned bit of evidence against that blind staggerer out there in the stable, not a shred of anything except that he can't see the day ahead to face the firing squad. You've got to die, he said suddenly, putting the glass down. Horse, it's your turn to die. This time it's not Penson or me but you, horse not man, you blank-eyed espial spying upon the secrets of eternity, you milky-eyed deserter. You're no good to any-one, he said, but he was looking at his own face in the sideboard mir-ror. Because this was the affair culminated at last between himself and the very fiber and substance of his going on, he did not begin thinking of Nancy until after the fifth glass of whiskey; and when he thought of her he put the glass stopper for the last time into the decanter and went at once, walking carefully but without any sem-blance of drunkenness, upstairs to his own bedroom and pulled open the bottom drawer of the dresser. From under the neatly folded cardigans, he took out the revolver and made sure that it was loaded, and then he put it into his jacket pocket. There were two more glasses of liquid left in the decanter and he drank them fast.

"That makes everything neat and tidy," he said, but when he stooped to retrieve the glass stopper which had dropped to the ground, his head spun slowly, so he helped himself erect again by holding to the table with one hand. Then he started walking, careful and trim in his squire's jacket, his silk kerchief folded on his neck, down the faintly steaming drive.

The sliding door was standing open beyond the wayfaring-tree and Mrs. Lombe and the young man in breeches were in the stable. They were not in the hunter's stall but talking together as they stood on the timber floor, and beyond the box's gate of hunter's quarters shone in the light. At the first sound of Candy's step on the wood, his wife turned her head with her sailor hat on it and said:

"This is Mr. Lombe, Mr. Harrison. I've had Mr. Harrison over this morning while Nan's up in London to do what has to be done."

Candy stood against the daylight in the door, a rather jaunty fig-ure with his hands in his jacket pockets, the back of the wrist and the left thumb showing, but this time the right thumb was out of sight. He nodded his head either in greeting or dismissal and teetered upwards, his legs planted wide apart, on his clean crepe soles.

"Where's Apby?" he said. "Does Apby know what's going on?"

"I sent him off early." She smiled a quick, tolerant, although impa-tient-seeming smile. "He's having the day off in Pellton. I told him I'd see the hunter got his midday meal. I haven't said anything to anybody. I just want to get it done as quickly and quietly as possible. It's not a pleasant job of work for anyone concerned. I had Richards take the mare to the village to have her shod."

"So there won't be any witnesses, not so much as a mare looking on, what?" said Candy, and now her eye on him altered as she began to suspect it. "Where do you intend to do it?" Candy said. Since that first step over the threshold he had not moved and his eyes had not shifted from her face, so if he had been asked then he could not have said whether the man called Harrison was short or tall, or what the color of his hair or what his age was, only that he remembered the

khaki breeches and the gaiters walking down the drive. "Where is justice to be meted out?" he said loudly, sardonically.

"Mr. Harrison is the huntsman from the local hunt," Mrs. Lombe said, saying the words pleasantly and exactly to him, as if it were a child's small, stubborn figure, not a man's and not her husband's, who stood teetering against the light. "He's been kind enough to offer to do it for us. He's an expert at it. I've arranged for the haulers to come at eleven and take the body away."

"Which body," said Candy, and now as good as if his breath had been wafted to her over the smell of clean horse and fresh bedding and clean mixture in the stable, she knew the bitter and unacceptable truth: that he was drunk, drunk at ten in the morning, that it was not curiosity that held him standing there haranguing but drunken opposition; not only drunk but drunk before lunch for a change and drunk before a stranger.

"Don't be an idiot, Candy," she said, laughing quickly, nervously, and glancing at Mr. Harrison in invitation to him to do the only possible thing and laugh. "You'd better go back to the house so Mr. Harrison can get on with it."

But Candy began crossing the stable now, walking blank-eyed, blank-faced, deliberately toward them, not swaying or deviating from the invisible line his intention had drawn, but walking carefully and deliberately at them as if they were no longer there now that he had started walking directly to where he wanted to go. They did not obstruct his way, but as he came they drew apart, each of them drawing to one side as a crowd might have drawn apart to allow the passage of a vehicle that ran on tracks and could not alter its course, and Candy passed between the two people who stared, the man in curiosity and the woman in wonder at him, and walked to the stall where the horse stood, its head hanging peacefully now across the gate. Candy took his left hand from his pocket and put it on the latch, and the horse threw his head up and Candy hesitated an instant, and then turned his head too and looked back at the two people standing, in their turn outlined and faceless, against the sunlight in the open stable-door.

"I just wanted to know," he said, almost imperceptibly swaying. "I just wanted to ask you before I go in there how Mr. Penson is, Mr. Har— I'd like to know."

The young man took a step or two towards him—young, thought Candy, seeing him for the first time now as he stood in relief against the yellowish brightness of the day outside, young only because the legs tapered in the breeches and the shoulders were broad and unsloping, for he could not see the features of the face or the color of the hair.

"I was just telling Mrs. Lombe," the man said in a strangely gentle, girl-like voice. "I was just telling her he died. He died last night."

"So an eye for an eye, a horse for a man, that's the way you look at it," said Candy, sardonically, but the whiskey was swinging hard and sickening in his head now and he held to the gate's wood for support. "A life for a life is what you think—" He saw Mrs. Lombe with the old sailor hat on coming towards him and he remembered I mustn't take my right hand out of my pocket until I'm ready. I can get the gate open with my left hand, like this, and now he had come through it and he stood on the oaten straw bedding by the horse now, and the gate was closed between him and his wife and the man she called Mr. Harrison. "He's so expert," he said, holding to the wood and pressing away from the horse's shoulder in the stall, "that he could probably do it without drawing the chalkline or do it with his eyes closed only he's not going to. The minute he takes out his revolver, I take out mine."

"Candy, come out," said Mrs. Lombe, but the conviction had lapsed from her voice. Candy was standing as far from the horse as he could get, the bordeaux-red silk kerchief around his throat because he hadn't shaved yet, the small of his back against the rough wood of the stall. "Please be reasonable, please come out," she said, but the power had gone from her. She stood with the straw hat pushed up off her forehead, seeking to say it with dignity.

"I'll come out when Nancy gets back," he said. "My little girl will come out here and she'll understand what I'm trying to do. She'll take shifts here with me, all summer if it has to be, hunger-strike, sleep-strike, drink-strike," he said, and at the last words the feeling of tears welled in him; and oh, heavens, heavens, thought the woman standing on the other side of the gate, what have I done that I should have to stand here before a stranger and hear him turning maudlin? What have

I done that it should have to happen like this? Oh, spare me. "And if you try to stop Nancy's marriage it'll be the same thing. I won't have you interfering with her and stopping her whatever she wants to do, lift a finger, go to a dance, have a horse of her own like—" And ah, unjust, unjust, thought the mother bitterly. Who was it picked out the clothes for her to go up to London, who was it had found the school for her in Florence last year? But there had been so many years of it now that it was for nothing else but the stranger's presence that she cared. "I'll wait here for my little girl," Candy went on saying in the same low-pitched and vagrant and scarcely defiant voice, "and you can't do anything to me because this time I've got the upper hand, for once I've got it. You've got the money but this time I tricked you, I fooled you, you can't field marshal me out of here, you can't major-domo me, you can't even bribe me—" Oh, sordid, sordid, thought the mother in grief as she looked at the small contorted flushed face, ageless and queer as a dwarf's, turning from one side to the other in fear of death and fear of life on the other side of the gate. In a moment she looked towards Mr. Harrison and whether the actual word was said or merely indicated, they both moved in simultaneous dignity and forbearance towards the door, crossing the timber to the threshold, and there the young man stood differentially to one side to let her pass before him out into the light. "You can go, but it won't make any difference to me," Candy called out, but then as the blind horse shifted a little nervously on the straw, he lowered his voice. "That's all right," he said, but when he looked at the massive shoulder and the strong hanging head his blood swooned in him. He stood leaning against the side of the stall, his hands in his pockets, seeking not to see the great, living, breathing beast with its eyes clogged blue and milky beneath the long, luxuriant lash, and then he took his left hand from the jacket's pocket and felt out the flask, and braced it against his ribs with his palm, the left hand's fingers fumbling off the cap. He did not stir his right hand but drew the cork out with his teeth and drank, and while he drank the horse brought his lowered head across the straw, the wide, soft nostrils seeking quiveringly for cognizance until the nose reached the shoes' tips and lipped across them, the monstrous, vacuous, ingesting suction of a snail mounting the ankles and the trousers to the jacket, and when the man brought his arm carefully down and his hand with the flask in it he dared move no longer but stood flattened against the stall's wood, waiting, the flask extended in his stricken hand. The horse's head lifted slowly, searchingly, the ears back, the hairs in the nostrils trembling in the blasts of breath, and now that the lips came blindly fumbling across his shoulder to his face, the cry of terror ripped from Candy's throat. "For Christ's sake!" he screamed, and the horse flung his head away in fright, swinging in the box until his quarters stood trembling across his buttocks and the points of his hocks. "I can't, I can't," Candy said under his breath and he began whimpering as he leaned against the boards. "I'm afraid, I have a right to be afraid," he said, but now that the horse had ceased to move he managed to cork the flask, his left hand shaking, and slip it into his back pocket. Then he stood quiet there for better than a quarter of an hour, his hands out of sight in his pockets, the dream of dauntlessness and sedulity vaguely augmenting and as vaguely waning, and at the last instant of fading reversing to a stronger, clearer, dizzier amplification. At the end of that little while, Mrs. Lombe and the huntsman came through the door and crossed the stable again.

"Mr. Harrison and I have been talking things over," she began in a measured, pleasant voice that must bring concurrence to logic in its wake. "Mr. Harrison thinks it might be very dangerous for you to stay in there with that horse. I explained to him the horse was not accustomed to being handled by you and he says that's where the great danger lies. It's strangers that worry them when there's anything wrong." He stood with the small of his back held against the boards, his eyes fixed sightless on the horse's rump and the long black tail that swept at intervals across it, and he did not speak. "If you're making this absurd scene for Nancy's sake," she went on, "I assure you she'd rather come home to find her ailing horse dead than to find her father in hospital—"

"Mr. Lombe," said the huntsman in his girl-like wounded voice, "it's scarcely taking the long view of things to—"

It was not Candy's passive opposition now that stopped them both, but without any warning he began to sing, lifting his head so that the back of it rested against the stall's boards, and his throat came

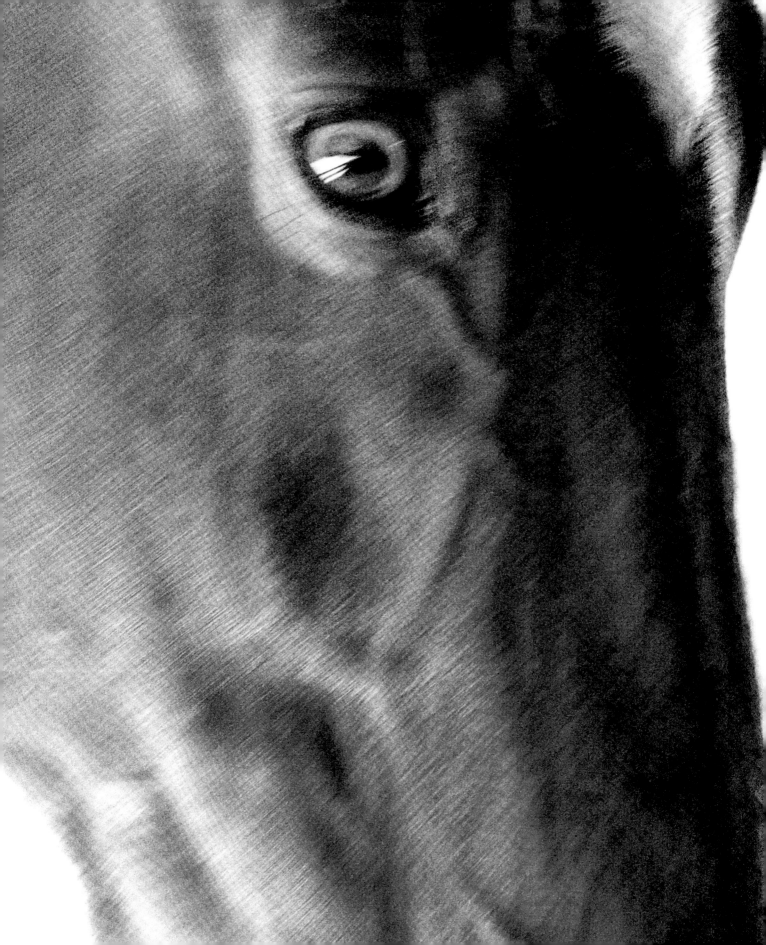

free of the silk kerchief as he sang loudlessly, tunelessly what words he remembered of what remnants of song he salvaged from the cahotage of terror and drink and despair.

"'I saw England's king from the top of a bus, He was riding in state so he didn't see us,'" he sang, bawling it out, and the horse flicked his ears. "'And though—oh, tra, tra, tra, te-de-dum—oh, by the Saxons we once were oppressed, I cheered, God forgive me, oh, God, oh, God, forgive me, I cheered with the rest, I—'"

Mrs. Lombe stepped a little nearer and spoke his name, and he glanced quickly at her and began at once:

"'I'm one of the ruins Cromwell knocked abaht a bit, I'm *one* of the ruins Cromwell knocked abaht a bit, oh, tra, la, la, la! Outside the Cromwell Arms last Saturday night I was one of the—'"

When the haulers came a little after eleven, Mrs. Lombe went to the door with dignity and sent them off, offering to pay them extra if they would be kind enough to come back in the afternoon. Candy had been singing: "'You remember young Peter O'Loughlin, of course? Well, here he is now at the head of the force! I met him one day while crossing the Strand—oh, God, oh, God bless him, he held up the street with one wave of his hand,'" but when he heard the men speaking outside and saw her go, proudly and discreetly as a lady might, to give them their directions, he turned his head towards the open door and shouted: "'Don't tell my mother I'm living in sin, Don't let the old folks—'" and they closed the door and left him to it. All through lunch time he stood motionless in the stall with the small of his back against the boards, and at two he had finished the whiskey. The horse had dropped his head and began eating his bedding for they had not watered or fed him since the morning meal. It was almost three o'clock when the haulers came back: he heard their horses and their voices outside in the sunlight, and then Mr. Harrison opened the stable door and he and Mrs. Lombe crossed the timber briskly together. At a little distance from the box they came to a stop.

"You must be very hungry," she said, standing there slightly in advance of the huntsman. "I had them put out some roastbeef sandwiches and beef on the veranda for you, so if you'll just come along—"

"No," said Candy, looking at the horse. "No, it's all right. You can't trick me." He was talking thick now, leaning against the side of the stall. "I'm waiting here for my little girl, I'm waiting, I'm on the side of civilization. This horse, he isn't a horse any moren any of us are horses, he's the forces of good against the forces of destruction, he's me, just as much me as artist, foreigner, just as much an outcast, he's freak and he's love, he's got something to do with love as it works out against—against this, this empire building and this susspression of the native, what you said the other night about Gandhi being so ugly himself, thin and his teeth out and his gums like the way you would talk about a horse, you said he was such a freak you didn't care what his beliefs were and didn't think he could have any looking like—well, this horse is against that sort of thing. He's for love. All right," he said, "now we've got it straight. This horse, he's all wrong and wherebyfore he's against everything that is your right and the world's right and Mr. Har— He's me by this time, and he's Nancy I think, or he's me and Nancy getting off to another country where everybody who speaks English is a foreigner, not only me. He's my horse, if he's a horse any more, and I bought him with your money, yes, all right, all rr-r-r-right, your money, but I bought something else at the same time, making the same purchase, my dear, something you haven't seen yet but it's there keeping me in the stable and in the stall until you get out of it and there doesn't have to be any explanation for him," mumbling it, half-crying it as he stood with his hands in his pockets staring at the horse's rump.

From: PORTRAIT OF THE ARTIST AS A YOUNG DOG

Dylan Thomas

*I*n the middle of the night I woke from a dream full of whips and lariats as long as serpents, and runaway coaches on mountain passes, and wide, windy gallops over cactus fields, and I heard the man in the next room crying, 'Gee-up!' and 'Whoa!' and trotting his tongue on the roof of his mouth…

'Whoa there, my beauties!' cried grandpa. His voice sounded very young and loud, and his tongue had powerful hooves, and he made his bedroom into a great meadow. I thought I would see if he was ill, or had set his bedclothes on fire, for my mother had said that he lit his pipe under the blankets, and had warned me to run to his help if I smelt smoke in the night. I went on tiptoe through the darkness to his bedroom door, brushing against the furniture and upsetting a candlestick with a thump. When I saw there was a light in the room I felt frightened, and as I opened the door I heard grandpa shout, 'Gee-up!' as loudly as a bull with a megaphone.

He was sitting straight up in bed and rocking from side to side as though the bed were on a rough road; the knotted edges of the counterpane were his reins; his invisible horses stood in a shadow beyond the bedside candle… At the sight of me, his hands dropped from the reins and lay blue and quiet, the bed stopped still on a level road, he muffled his tongue into silence, and the horses drew softly up.

'Is there anything the matter, Grandpa?' I asked, though the clothes were not on fire. His face in the candlelight looked like a ragged quilt pinned upright on the black air and patched all over with goat-beards.

He stared at me mildly. Then he blew down his pipe, scattering the sparks and making a high, wet dog-whistle of the stem, and shouted: 'Ask no questions.'

After a pause, he said slyly: 'Do you ever have nightmares, boy?'

I said: 'No.'

'Oh, yes, you do,' he said.

I said I was woken by a voice that was shouting to horses.

'What did I tell you?' he said. 'You eat too much. Who ever heard of horses in a bedroom?'

He fumbled under his pillow, brought out a small tinkling bag, and carefully untied its strings. He put a sovereign in my hand, and said: 'Buy a cake.' I thanked him and wished him goodnight.

As I closed my bedroom door, I heard his voice crying loudly and gaily, "Gee-up! gee-up!" and the rocking of the travelling bed.

NINE HORSES

Billy Collins

For my birthday,
my wife gave me nine horse heads,
ghostly photographs on squares of black marble,
nine squares set in one large square,
a thing so heavy that the artist himself
volunteered to hang it
from a wood beam against a white stone wall.

Pale heads of horses in profile
as if a flashcube had caught them walking in the night.

Pale horse heads
that overlook my reading chair,
the eyes so hollow they must be weeping,

the mouths so agape they could be dead—
the photographer standing over them
on a floor of straw, his black car parked by the stable door.

Nine white horses,
or one horse the camera has multiplied by nine.

It hardly matters, such sadness is gathered here
in their long white faces
so far from the pasture and the cube of sugar—
the face of St. Bartholomew, the face of St. Agnes.

Odd team of horses,
pulling nothing,
look down on these daily proceedings.

Look down upon this table and these glasses,
the furled napkins,
the evening wedding of the knife and fork.

Look down like a nine-headed god
and give us a sign of your displeasure
of your gentle forbearance
so that we may rejoice in the error of our ways.

Look down on this ring
of candles flickering under your pale heads.

Let your suffering eyes
and your anonymous deaths
be the bridle that keeps us from straying from each other

be the cinch that fastens us to the belly of each day

as it gallops away, hooves sparking into the night.

From: SPARKS

Laura Chester

Call me wall me Zucchero. (*Catch him if you can*. Too far gone for halter, lead or lunge line now. Once ready steed, he stands apart, steps or stumbles all agog, ranging on Rose Hill, wandering down the road, a steady plod before the bridge that he's afraid to cross. I stand beside you, Zucchero, and watch the waters gush—the earth is juicy, spilling, rushing from its slit—the lance that pierced the side of flesh, and out ran water out ran blood—alive now in this gully, so much so good to munch. And here I come, your leisure, with rubber pail and box of sugar, calling you, "My Sweetness"—trusting, waiting, listing, leaning, moonless, blotted evening. Grass smell fresh upon his breath, the taste of brown lump sugar. He lets the rope go round his neck, loosely leading him along beside the excavator. He lets me take him over. His mouth is filled with coated oats, sweetness his last supper. I kiss him then and taste his tears. His eye is wide, his head goes up— and suddenly he tumbles. He stumbles yet he flies! Bless him now with petals, holy oil and petals—(*Close his open eye*.

From: IN PRAISE OF HORSES

Mark Spragg

I knelt by his ears and lifted his head and scooted my knees under it and laid the broad thick bone of his skull against my thighs. He did not struggle. I closed my eyes and prayed for the strength to lift him and carry him to safety, and felt no stronger, and began to cry again. I bent my mouth to the soft, furred cup of his ear and whispered that I was sorry. I knew it did not matter to him. I knew that it mattered only to me. I said that I was sorry again.

I stood away from him and straightened the blanket on his neck and shoulder and walked back to the fire and squatted with my back to the flames until my ass warmed. The black night pressed down like water. My chest felt heavy. I had to stand to get a breath.

I sat back against the saddle and pulled the slickers over me and slept. There was only the sound of the fire, and in my sleep I dreamed that I lived on the back of a horse. In the dream I was fully grown. I was a naked, gaunt, and happy man, and I never stood down upon the earth. When I was tired I lay along the horse's back to sleep. When I was thirsty the rains came and I opened my mouth and drank. I was filled with rainwater and ozone. I draped forward on the horse's neck to rest. My arms hung to the sides of his neck. My hands clenched and relaxed. I breathed into his coarse, dark mane. My lungs filled with the salted, sweetmeat taste of the horse on which I lived.

In my dream I stood on the horse's rump and pissed a yellow arc into the air and my head fell back and I screamed into the vault of the black night sky, and turned and walked to his withers and sat.

He was a pinto horse, dark eyed, dark nostriled, dark stockinged with one white hoof, front left, slightly softer than the darker three. Each foot struck out a single note as he stepped to graze. He made music as he ran. The lighter hoof slapping the earth in a tone shallower than the other three.

I sat upright on that horse and held my arms high like the armatures of long, slim wings and leaned slightly forward, and he broke into a run. I could feel the cool air tighten my flesh. I could feel the horse grow hot and lathered, and I knew that when a horse is running flat-out toward the curve of the earth that all four feet, regardless of color, leave the ground at once. I closed my eyes. I heard us skip into the air and touch the earth again, and I knew that it was in those suspended moments, relaxed from effort, that the rider and the ridden are afforded, in that instant, and in the next, and the next after that, the sight of God. I saw God looking at me in the dream and knew it was a horse I had to thank.

I woke in the early light. A gray jay stepped through the gray ash of the fire, and when I kicked off the slickers he rose into a pine and chattered. The slickers were stiff with frost. I took off my hat and beat the frost from its crown and stomped and shook. I expected to be alone. I felt alone. I expected to find a dead horse, to shoulder my saddle and start down the trail. I didn't look up until I was close to Sky. I almost jumped back when he lifted his head. He focused hard on me and tucked his legs and rolled onto them and stood. He swayed and caught himself.

I bridled him and led him to the creek, and he sucked at the water for a long time. I took a step upstream and knelt and cupped water on my face and drank. The ground and trees were dirty white with frost. It looked as though we stood inside the skeleton of a cloud. I felt better than the boy who had gone to sleep. I felt older than the boy who'd nearly killed his horse.

From: THE LIVING

Annie Dillard

*Th*e sky came carousing down around him. He saw the sun drenching the green westward islands and battering a path down the water. He saw the town before him to the south, where the trestle lighted down. Then far on the Nooksack plain to the east, he saw a man walking. The distant figure was turning pea rows under in perfect silence. He was dressed in horse's harness and he pulled the plow. His feet trod his figure's long blue shadow, and the plow cut its long blue shadow in the ground. The man turned back as if to look along the furrow, to check its straightness. Clare saw again, on the plain farther north, another man; this one walked behind a horse and turned the green ground under. Then before him on the trestle over the water he saw the earth itself walking, the earth walking darkly as it always walks in every season: it was plowing the men under, and the horses, and the plows.

DONNA DeMARI has been shooting fashion and fine arts photography since the late seventies. Her work has appeared in many top European magazines, including *Vogue, Elle,* and *Marie Claire.* A show of her horse photographs, "Flying Mane," was held at the SAS Gallery. Her photographs were included in the book of selected prose-poems, *Sparks,* by Laura Chester. DeMari was also the photographer for Holy Personal, published by Indiana University Press.
 www.donnademari.com.

ACKNOWLEDGMENTS

Bagnold, Enid. Excerpt from *National Velvet*. Copyright © 1935 William Morrow. Reprinted with permission of the estate of Enid Bagnold.

Boyle, Kay. "The Crazy Hunter" by Kay Boyle, from *Fifty Stories*, copyright © 1980 by Kay Boyle. Reprinted by permission of New Directions Publishing Corp.

Bukowski, Charles. "12 Minutes to Post" from *Betting on the Muse: Poems & Stories* by Charles Bukowski. Copyright © 1996 by Linda Lee Bukowski. Reprinted by permission of HarperCollins Publishers.

Chester, Laura. Excerpt from: *Free Rein*. Copyright © 1988 by Laura Chester. Reprinted with permission of Burning Deck Press.

Chester, Laura. "Time to Put Zucchero Down," from *Sparks*. Copyright © 2002 by Laura Chester. Reprinted with permission of the publisher, The Figures.

Collins, Billy. "Nine Horses," from *Nine Horses* by Billy Collins. Copyright © 2002 by Billy Collins. Used by permission of SLL/Sterling Lord Literistic, Inc.

Creeley, Robert. Excerpt from "Breath," from *Life and Death,* copyright © 1998 by Robert Creeley. Reprinted by permission of New Directions Publishing Corp.

Dillard, Annie. Excerpt from *The Living* by Annie Dillard. Copyright © 1992 by Annie Dillard. Reprinted by permission of HarperCollins Publishers.

Dinesen, Isak. Excerpt from *Out of Africa* by Isak Dinesen, copyright © 1937 by Random House, Inc. and renewed 1965 by Rungstedlundfonden. Used by permission of Random House, Inc.

Dixon, Jeanne. "River Girls" first published by *Northern Lights* magazine, editor Deb Chow. Copyright © 1990 by Jeanne Dixon. Reprinted by permission of the author.

Edson, Russell. "A Redundancy of Horses," copyright © Russell Edson. Reprinted by permission of the author.

Esquivel, Laura. Excerpt from *Like Water for Chocolate* by Laura Esquivel, copyright Translation © 1992 by Doubleday, a division of Random House, Inc. Used by permission of Doubleday, a division of Random House, Inc.

Gallagher, Tess. Excerpt from *The Lover of Horses*, copyright © 1982 Harper & Row, Graywolf Press. Reprinted by permission of the author.

Gerstler, Amy. "Horses and Girls" copyright © Amy Gerstler. Reprinted by permission of the author.

Giono, Jean. Excerpt from *Joy of Man's Desiring* by Jean Giono. Copyright © 1980 by Aline Giono. Reprinted by permission of Counterpoint, a member of Perseus Books, LLC.

Grealy, Lucy. Excerpt from: *Autobiography of a Face* by Lucy Grealy. Copyright © 1994 by Lucy Grealy. Reprinted by permission of Houghton Mifflin Company. All rights reserved.

Lifshin, Lyn. Poems from *The Licorice Daughter, My Year with Ruffian*, copyright © 2005 by Lyn Lifshin (Texas Review Press. English Dept. Sam Houston State University, Huntville, Texas). Reprinted by permission of the author and publisher.

Logghe, Joan. "Confessor Horse," copyright © Joan Logghe. Reprinted by permission of the author.

Midkiff, Mary. Excerpt from *She Flies Without Wings: How Horses Touch a Woman's Soul* by Mary Midkiff, copyright © 2001 by Mary D. Midkiff. Used by permission of Dell Publishing, a division of Random House, Inc.

Podhajsky, Alois. Excerpt from *My Horses, My Teachers* by Col. Alois Podhajsky. Originally published by Doubleday & Company, 1968; republished by Trafalgar Square Publishing (N. Pomfret, Vermont). Used by permission of Trafalgar Square Publishing.

Salter, James. "Twenty Minutes," from *Dusk and Other Stories*. Copyright © 1988 by James Salter. Reprinted by permission of SLL/Sterling Lord Literistic, Inc.

Saroyan, William. "The Summer of the Beautiful White Horse," from *My Name is Aram*, copyright © 1938 by Harcourt Trade Publishers. Reprinted by permission of the Trustees of Leland Stanford Junior University.

Sassoon, Siegfried. Excerpt from *Memoirs of a Fox-Hunting Man*. In public domain.

Shaffer, Peter. Excerpt from: *Equus and Shrivings* by Peter Shaffer. Copyright © 1973, 1974 by Peter Shaffer; copyright renewed © 2001, 2002 by Peter Shaffer. Reprinted with the permission of Scribner, an imprint of Simon & Schuster Adult Publishing Group.

Smiley, Jane. Excerpt from *Horse Heaven* by Jane Smiley, copyright © 2000 by Jane Smiley. Used by permission of Alfred A. Knopf, a division of Random House, Inc.

Spragg, Mark. Excerpt from "In Praise of Horses" from *Where Rivers Change Direction*. Copyright © 1999 by Mark Spragg. Reprinted by permission of the author.

Thomas, Dylan. Excerpt from *Portrait of the Artist as a Young Dog,* copyright © 1940 by New Directions Publishing Corp. Reprinted by permission of New Directions Publishing Corp.

Tremain, Rose. Excerpt from *Music and Silence* by Rose Tremain. Copyright © 1999 by Rose Tremain. Reprinted by permission of Farrar, Straus and Giroux, LLC.

Wright, James. "A Blessing" from *Collected Poems*, copyright © 1971 by James Wright and reprinted by permission of Wesleyan University Press.

Yoors, Jan. Excerpt from *The Gypsies*, copyright © 1967 by Jan Yoors. Reprinted by permission of Waveland Press, Inc. (Long Grove, IL; Waveland Press, Inc., 1967 [reissued 1987]). All rights reserved.

Zarzyski, Paul. "The Bucking Horse Moon" from *All This Way for the Short Ride, Poems*, copyright © 1996 by Paul Zarzyski. Published by the Museum of New Mexico Press. Reprinted by permission of the author. All rights reserved.